Editorial director Jane O'Shea
Creative director Helen Lewis
Designer Lawrence Morton
Project editor Lisa Pendreigh
Editorial assistant Andrew Bayliss
Picture researcher Hilary Davies and Louise Edgworth for FMS
Production director Vincent Smith
Production controller Ruth Deary

This paperback edition first published in 2008 by Quadrille Publishing Limited, Alhambra House, 27–31 Charing Cross Road, London WC2H 0LS
www.quadrille.co.uk

Text © 2006 Nicholas Foulkes
Design and layouts © Quadrille Publishing Limited

All rights reserved. No part of this book may be reproduced, stored in a retrieval system or transmitted in any form or by any means, electronic, electrostatic, magnetic tape, mechanical, photocopying, recording or otherwise, without the prior permission in writing of the publisher.

The rights of Nicholas Foulkes to be identified as the author of this work have been asserted by him in accordance with the Copyright, Designs and Patents Act 1988.

British Library Cataloguing-in-Publication Data: a catalogue record for this book is available from the British Library.

ISBN: 978 184400 601 4

Printed and bound in China

The Bentley Boys, winning drivers of the 1929 Le Mans (page 1).

A Bentley hurtles past barricades placed along the street (previous page), driven by Beris Harcourt Wood in a 1929 road race.

W.O. Bentley, founder of the eponymous marque, in his racing D.F.P (right) during the 1914 T.T. race on the Isle of Man.

Nicholas Foulkes

The Bentley Era

the fast and furious story of the fabulous Bentley Boys

QUADRILLE

6 INTRODUCTION

8 PART ONE: THE BEGINNINGS OF BENTLEY

58 PART TWO: AN UNCERTAIN FUTURE

92 PART THREE: ON THE ROAD TO GLORY

120 PART FOUR: THE GOLDEN YEARS

180 EPILOGUE

184 NOTES

187 INDEX

191 ACKNOWLEDGEMENTS

Foreword

It was a pleasant evening in the summer of 2000 and I had just driven, rather more rapidly than was prudent, from Paris to a charming château a few kilometres outside Le Mans. It was the weekend of the famous 24 hour race and I had been part of a high-speed motorcade of Bentleys – vintage and modern – that had left the courtyard of the British Embassy on the Rue du Faubourg Saint-Honoré and battled its way through Paris's Friday night traffic. Now we were relaxing over dinner the night before the race.

I was sitting on a table dominated by members of the Bentley Drivers' Club, and by the time the cheese had been cleared away and replaced by cognac and coffee the conversation had turned to what was regarded as the Bentley era; a time during the 1920s when W.O. (as Walter Owen Bentley preferred to be known) presided over his eponymous automotive marque and the cars that carried his name were driven with élan by the feckless, reckless, gilded youth of the years between the Treaty of Versailles and the Wall Street Crash. For about an hour I listened as members of the BDC debated the characters and merits of the Bentley Boys, who raced and won time after time after time during the 1920s for W.O. and for England. From the conversation that evening it would appear that the Bentley Boys partied as hard as they drove, perhaps harder.

But while tempting to view that age as one extended party, it was in reality a complex time; economic and political uncertainty were tempered by considerable scientific and technological advances. Change was all around and yet the old order, particularly in England, seemed to stand solid. At the beginning of the 1920s, many of the fortunes of the aristocracy and the great nineteenth-century mercantile families were still intact.

In many ways the behaviour of this privileged elite seems irresponsible and perhaps even offensive by the standards of the twenty-first century. However, while researching this book I discovered different sides to the Bentley Boys, making them altogether much more interesting characters than two-dimensional fun-loving motor racers; beneath the suave lady-killing exteriors and Mayfair manners were thinking, feeling people who believed that the privileges they enjoyed came with a sense of responsibility, duty and a desire to enhance national prestige. Of course these were not selfless saints, but rich young men, their appetite for the good life sharpened by the horrors of the war just gone and the looming shadows of the one to come. Their lives were an evocative mix of fear, fun, exhilaration, intoxication, private poignancy and public glamour.

As soon as I heard some of the stories of the Bentley Boys that warm summer evening at the beginning of this century, I knew I wanted to write their story and I hope that it is an enjoyable one; it does not pretend to be a thorough biographical study of these men, more of an extended snapshot of extraordinary men who lived (and died) during an extraordinary time.

This book would never have been written without the support of Bentley Motors and its chairman Dr Franz-Josef Paefgen, whose enthusiastic anglophilia would have delighted the Bentley Boys. It was Janette Green who shepherded this project through the Byzantine corporate structure of Bentley, and having put in the hard work to guarantee the publication of the book left to work for a rival British automotive marque, leaving the project in the capable hands of Mark Tennant.

In the course of researching this book, many individuals and organisations were of immense help, John Konig generously allowed us to make use of rare photographs of his old family home, Ardenrun, which was sold to Barnato. It was also John Konig who put me onto Simon Kidston, who generously allowed me the run of his fascinating and at times moving family papers. Diana Barnato Walker was a delightful person to spend time with and I am grateful for her unique insights into the character of her father. The Vintage Sports Car Club put their resources at my disposal and could not have been more helpful. Thanks are also due to the Earl of March, Robert Benjafield, James Buxton, Hugo Kidston, Cath Kidston, Michael Russell, Richard Charlesworth and the Bentley Drivers' Club.

As ever I must thank my agent Luigi Bonomi, a friend as a well as a guide and my remarkable research assistant Sophie Robinson, who happily for me is an enthusiastic driver of a vintage sports car and has acquitted herself well at one or two hill climbs. Throughout everything Quadrille has proved a patient and encouraging publisher and I am grateful to Jane O'Shea and Lisa Pendreigh for their tolerance and kindness.

PART ONE

The beginnings of Bentley

Chapter One

Framed in the workshop

in a mews just off Baker Street that October morning in 1919 stood the formidable figure of the hospital matron. Feet planted far apart, hands firmly on hips; the grim set of this early twentieth-century health professional's features spoke eloquently enough.

doorway of the

THE BEGINNINGS OF BENTLEY

A 3 Litre outside the Bentley workshop (previous page); the chassis is ready to be sent to the coachbuilders to receive its body.

W.O. Bentley, portrait from May 1914.

The solemn, taciturn and neat young man, his hair parted precisely on the left and greased into place, affected to be nonplussed as he looked up from the work in which he had been engrossed all morning. "Go and see what she wants", he said to Captain Gallop, standing at his side.[1]

Gallop, a recently demobilised officer in the Royal Flying Corps and pre-First World War Brooklands racing driver, had been working with this serious young man since the summer and had come to understand him quite well: Walter Owen Bentley was a man of few words but immense industry, which he had expended on the development of a new 3-litre motorcar engine.

After a few short months of frenzied work, Bentley had designed and assembled the components. During the summer and early autumn of 1919, a small band of mechanics had been carrying mysterious bits of metal up the stairs and into the sparsely equipped workshop with its pedal-powered grindstone and bench drill. As the summer wore on and the mechanics got to know each other, banter passed between the upper and lower storeys via a large hole in the floor through which heavier items were raised and lowered.

At length their work was done and the engine was ready to start. A real sense of expectation and tension grew as those who had helped the solemn young W.O. (Bentley disliked the name Walter and preferred to be called by his initials) over recent months crowded into the small building to see if their hard work and faith in this painfully shy but mechanically gifted young man had been justified. A knot of about eight people gathered around the engine. "I was surprised that W.O. allowed so many people to be present", recalled one young man who was there that morning, "as he had an intense dislike for anything in the way of an exhibition".[2] But an exhibition it was, with the star of the show, the engine, looking 'very new and proud standing alone on its wooden trestle'.[3]

Among those visiting the mews that morning was W.O.'s brother and business partner, Colonel Horace Milner Bentley, who had brought his dog with him. H.M., as the Colonel was better known, told one of the mechanics who had been working all summer on the new engine to look after his pet while he went upstairs to be present at the birth. Somewhat put out – he was not going to look after a dog while the engine he had worked on was about to start up – the mechanic tied the canine to the banisters and peered up through the hole in the ceiling, craning his neck in the hope of seeing something.

"She was a bit of a pig to start; they had to try all sorts of things", he later recalled.[4] This bald statement fails to convey the icy atmosphere in the upper room, where the 'silence could be felt'.[5] Not a word was uttered. W.O.'s features darkened. Anticlimax grew into concern as the engine stubbornly failed to start. 'There was an uneasy shuffling of feet,

CHAPTER ONE

Not a word was uttered. W.O.'s features darkened. Anticlimax grew into concern as the engine stubbornly failed to start.

and only a well-directed kick on the shin prevented one misguided know-all from offering advice. Then suddenly W.O. spoke. Addressing no one in particular, he said: "Benzole![6] Get me some benzole!"[7] A can of the 'evil smelling spirit'[8] was found and poured into and over the engine with about a pint of the stuff splashing on the floor for good measure.

"They sent out for Benzole in the end," recollected the mechanic, "but I also remember Clive Gallop asking about trying some ether; whether they did actually use it I don't know, but it was mentioned. I remember that distinctly because I didn't know then that ether could be used in that way."[9]

Eventually there was silence as W.O attempted to bring his creation to life; some adjustment of the valve timing was required, a little bit of fiddling with the carburettor and then… a loud explosion and the eight or so people gathered upstairs were treated to a bright yellow flash as the engine started to roar. "There was this terrific belch from the short exhaust manifold, and the whole place shook. Of course, once they got it running everybody shouted – delighted – and they simply kept it running then. It was a really beautiful sound."[10] As his friends and employees cheered, W.O. allowed himself the luxury of a slight smile as he listened to the sweet music of the engine.

However not everyone appreciated the lusty roar of the first-ever, 3-litre Bentley. The matron was clearly far from amused. Captain Gallop detached himself from the small knot of men standing entranced around the engine, which was still making a very gratifying din and filling the mews with thick blue fumes. After a little while, Gallop sauntered back, a smile playing around his lips. Cupping his hands and placing them to W.O.'s ear, he shouted to make himself heard above the bellow of the three-inch exhaust and the banshee-like scream of the straight tooth gears. "She says we're to stop this row at once. There's a man ill next door."[11]

But W.O. Bentley was simply too busy to pay her any attention; he had no intention of stopping his engine, *his own engine*, now that it had spluttered into life. "Tell her to go away", he instructed brusquely, while those men around the engine who had heard the exchange nodded their assent.[12] Many of them had served in the Royal Flying Corps during the First World War; they had seen friends plummet to their deaths in burning aircraft and had flown over the carnage of the trenches every day.

Captain Clive Gallop taking a pitstop whilst competing in an **Aston Martin** in the French **Grand Prix**, Strasbourg, 16 July 1922.

THE BEGINNINGS OF BENTLEY

W.O. Bentley, at 80, in Chagford Street, formerly New Street Mews, the site of the first Bentley workshop.

With the roar of that first Bentley engine the twentieth century can be said to have truly begun. One of the greatest sports cars was born.

Death had become quotidian. Even after the war had stopped, death had not; the appalling pandemic of Spanish flu had carried off many whom war had spared, among them W.O. Bentley's wife. For those who survived, theirs was the generation that scorned death, ridiculed it, and lived accordingly.

"A happy sound to die to – the exhaust roar of the first 3-litre Bentley engine", someone later muttered.[13] And for all Bentley knew or cared, the man under the matron's care might have been dying, but in here he, W.O., was giving birth ... not just to a 3-litre, four-cylinder engine, but to an automotive marque that would become a symbol of the coming decade and its *carpe diem* values.

It was less than a year since the guns along the trenches had fallen silent and only a few months earlier that the Allies in Versailles had imposed terms on a vanquished Germany. The nineteenth-century order and its values had been swept away; and with the roar of that first Bentley engine the twentieth century can be said to have truly begun. One of the greatest sports cars was born. Speed, money, glamour, chivalry, patriotism, daring... the Bentley marque would come to embody all these things. But just for the moment it was one engine in a smoke-filled London mews.

Over the next couple of months the engine was worked on and then lowered by block and tackle through the hole in the workshop floor, manhandled into a chassis and bolted down. Just as the chassis had been assembled, Gallop turned up and was understandably excited to see the vehicle taking shape complete with radiator. The light, experimental body was standing at the side. "Well, it could be driven, if the body was put on", said the former air ace, and with that, the body was lifted over the steering

CHAPTER ONE

wheel and dropped into place, and held there by a few hastily applied clips.¹⁴ A plank of wood was found and placed on the chassis; and with the added comfort of an old cushion as driver's seat, the first Bentley made its way gingerly out of the mews and into motoring history.

Gallop was delighted: it felt wonderful, the brakes worked, and then, all of a sudden, he found himself being pulled into the chassis. 'Suddenly it was realised that the carden-shaft had got hold of the tail of his dust-coat and was pulling him down on to it: his coat went z-i-p! – and it ripped right up the back.'¹⁵ The car was stopped, allowing the unfortunate Captain Gallop to be unwound and separated from the vehicle. The car was then returned to the mews. That afternoon W.O. came to look at his eponymous car; only years later did he find out he was not the first person to drive it.

W.O. driving the EXP1, the first car to bear his name, in January 1920.

CHAPTER TWO

the seeds of it

all had, of course, been sown during the war',

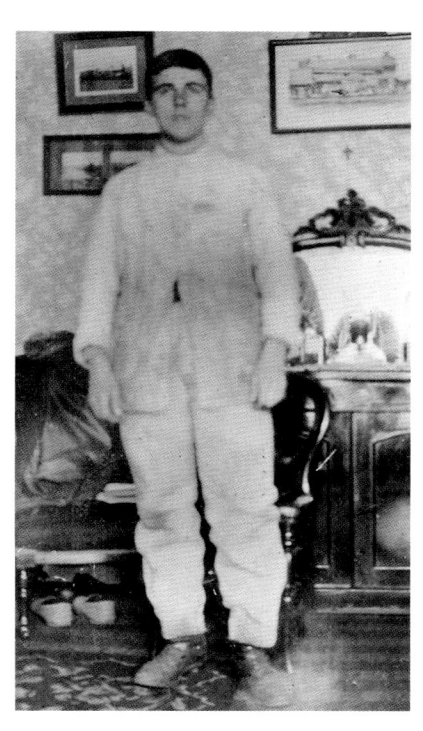

wrote W.O. in his 1958 autobiography, of his decision to start his own automotive marque.[16] It could be argued that the seeds had been sown much earlier. As a child the main traits of W.O.'s character began to be apparent: the shyness, the remote, withdrawn nature and the fascination with mechanical objects.

THE BEGINNINGS OF BENTLEY

Born in 1888 into a large family, made comfortable by, among other things, a legacy from his maternal grandfather, W.O. remembers his childhood thus: 'In that fully populated, typically Victorian house I succeeded in being quiet and rather independent. I imagine myself at the age of five or six deeply involved in pulling something painstakingly to pieces, or equally painstakingly putting it together again, either in the big nursery we all shared or in my bedroom.'[17] His favourite toys were a stationary steam engine and a clockwork train set.

The railway first engaged the mechanical mind of W.O. He left Clifton College at sixteen to become an apprentice on the Great Northern Railway. Conditions were tough: he worked a sixty-hour week, was teased for his southern accent and called a snob. Tenacity was also part of his character so he stuck at it, and found himself on the footplate working as a fireman.

It was during this time that he became keen on motorcycles, for the scope and freedom they offered a young man. In 1906 he purchased his first machine, a belt-driven, 3-h.p. Quadrant – 'the first mechanically propelled vehicle any Bentley had ever owned'.[18] His brothers H.M. and A.W. soon followed, buying a Quadrant and a Triumph respectively. W.O. and A.W. then entered the London to Edinburgh Trial in 1906, each winning a gold medal, even though W.O. was hampered by a dead ignition and flat tyre.

By 1908 W.O. was astride a 5-h.p. Rex, winning gold medals in two long-distance trials from London to Plymouth and back and to Land's End and back. He entered the 1909 Tourist Trophy (T.T.) on a different Rex – a 3-$\frac{1}{2}$ Speed Model – but skidded out of the race without even completing the first lap. Later that year he entered a one-hour race at Brooklands and he began to reveal his engineering genius; a racing modification he had made to improve reliability and lubrication was later incorporated by Rex in their standard production models. Later in 1909 he won a gold medal at the Six Days Trial, which took place over the Welsh hills. In 1910 he entered the Isle of Man T.T. with an Indian, and managed one lap – with a time of 19 minutes and 27 seconds – before being put out of the race by tyre failure. However, the following day he logged the fastest time up the Snaefell hill climb.

His last competitive ride was back at Brooklands in the One Hour T.T., where he finished second. By that time he had completed his apprenticeship on the railways and, after five years of manual labour, decided that the

W.O. on a 1909 Rex motorcycle (previous page, above); the company were later to incorporate some of W.O.'s own modifications into their standard production models.

Even as a youngster, W.O. took engineering seriously; while the pictures on the wall show the trains he was fascinated by, his overalls – while not polite Edwardian dress – testify to his enthusiasm (previous page, below).

1909 Spring Motor Cycle handicap at Brooklands (above), in which W.O. competed on his Rex.

W.O. Bentley in his racing D.F.P. during the 1914 T.T. race on the Isle of Man (opposite), in which he came last.

The nine-cylinder BR2 aero engine designed by W.O.; along with its predecessor the BR1, this engine successfully powered several wartime aircraft including the Sopwith Camel.

CHAPTER TWO

railways were not for him. Instead he wanted to join the motor trade: a letter to a motoring journalist friend resulted in a job at a taxi firm.

He soon wanted more. 'The attraction of the power and speed of the motor-car, the realization of the independence and the means to take you over a great distance that it offered, came to me at a period of growing self-confidence and coincided with a keen wish to make more money and to be my own master.'[19]

The opportunity soon presented itself in the shape of a small French sports car known as the D.F.P. (Doriet, Flandrin et Parent). The concession for this nippy, well-made vehicle, for which W.O. saw great potential, was owned by two comical characters; Lecoq, who was more interested in Vuitton Trunks, his other business; and a caricature cavalry officer called Major Fernie, 'complete with aggressive ginger moustache'.[20] Neither man knew much about selling cars, and in a short while W.O. and H.M. had bought them out. Labour at the new firm of Bentley & Bentley was split between H.M., who worked on sales at the Hanover Street showroom, and W.O., who moved into a rented coach-house in New Street Mews off Upper Baker Street, where seven years later the Benzole-drenched 3-litre Bentley engine would explode into life.

The 12–15-h.p. D.F.P. was the car W.O. Bentley saw as the star of a three-model range. In continental Europe, this was a solid four-seater, but he had other plans: with a tuned engine he felt it would make a good sports car. He proved as much on his first outing as a competitive driver, piloting it to victory in its class at the Aston Clinton Hill Climb, in record time, with his fiancée Leonie in the passenger seat.

W.O. and his brother agreed that competitive driving was a viable way of getting the car noticed and entered a D.F.P. racing model in various competitions of different kinds, while performance was improved by fitting aluminium pistons. By the beginning of 1914 things were looking good – he had married his hill-climb passenger and looked forward to promoting the increasingly popular D.F.P. sports car, marketed a trifle misleadingly as 'The Car That Won't Wear Out'[21] – when the Great War intervened.

The effects of the First World War on the world when W.O. was winning races in his tweaked D.F.P. cannot be underestimated. Before 1914 life was predictable and ordered. Europe was ruled not by kings but by emperors: one in St Petersburg, one in Berlin, another in Vienna and, of course, the King Emperor George V in London. Before the end of the decade, three of these unassailable leaders had been toppled, social order had been threatened, Russia was fighting a cruel civil war, Germany laboured under punitive reparations and the Austro–Hungarian Empire (itself the remainder of the ancient Holy Roman Empire) had been broken up into a patchwork of newly invented countries. By the time the slaughter ended in November 1918, millions were dead.

W.O. had spent the war developing aero engines: Bentley Rotary One and Bentley Rotary Two (B.R.1 and B.R.2). As part of his work he would take tours of the airfields, even taking to the air. Once, taking tea on the ground with a fighter ace, they were strafed by Manfred von Richthofen, the infamous 'Red Baron', whose Fokker tri-plane was responsible for 80 downed Allied aircraft. To avoid the Baron's bullets, W.O. jumped into a canal. On the Baron's second run, another man, Petty Officer 'Nobby' Clarke, splashed into the canal next to W.O. It is interesting to note that a Bentley Rotary engine powered the Sopwith Camel, flown by Captain A.R. Brown, that shot down Manfred von Richthofen on 22 April 1918 during the second Battle of the Somme. "I almost felt a pang of regret when Brown in a Camel, powered by one of our B.R.1s, caught him at last", recalled W.O.

During the war the fledgling business of Bentley & Bentley kept going thanks to its piston business and the occasional trading of second-hand D.F.P.s. It even attempted to sell a paraffin-powered tractor. One day towards the end of 1918, H.M. came into the office in civilian clothes and announced, "we must buy every second-hand D.F.P. we can lay our hands on. There's going to be a boom."[22] Indeed the firm was soon buying and selling cars of all makes, but with his return from the war W.O. wanted to do more than sell other people's cars. 'I had decided that it just wasn't going to be enough for me to return to the agency business, profitable though it had been, and would be again. The creative instinct is strong in most engineers', he wrote of his return to civilian life, 'so I had to produce my own car'.[23] On 20 January 1919 W.O. sat down with two associates in a small office in Conduit Street to design the first Bentley.

As plans progressed and became more concrete, old friends from the war were called on. Clive Gallop was one, and the man with whom W.O. shared a canal while under fire from the Red Baron was another. 'Dear Clarke' ran a letter from the secretary of the newly formed Bentley Motors on 9 July 1919. 'Capt. Bentley would like to see you here, and I shall be pleased if you will let me know when you can get up to town.' The formal business dealt with, the letter adopted a much warmer, more 'chocks away' style invoking the wartime camaraderie. 'I am working with Capt. Bentley and would like to see you in the show. The job which is open would suit a man who could rouse as much enthusiasm as we had in No 4 Squadron, and I hope you will be able to fix matters up.'[24] It might as well have signed off with a 'pip pip', but instead the more formal 'Yours sincerely' was adopted. A few days later, Nobby Clarke was part of the 'show' at the mews. And so it went on.

Bentley was far from the only man trying to build a car and a reputation in those heady, optimistic first months after the war. 'If one looks at the motoring magazines of 1919 and 1920 it was obvious that there were dozens of little companies who had decided to make cars', wrote one engineer of the period, adding darkly 'but it didn't take long for many of them to go bankrupt'.[25]

Bentley Motors had got off to a flying start; it had an engine in a chassis and by 26 December 1919 W.O. was tearing up and down Brockley Hill in the 3-litre car that had tried to chew up Captain Gallop. But in such uncertain times, just how long would it last?

CHAPTER TWO

W.O. in his D.F.P. racer, the car that he marketed with the claim that it would not wear out.

Chapter Three

1 If Bentley Motors was to succeed

in the tough and competitive environment of the 1920s it would need plenty of good publicity, and in those days one of the most famous motoring journalists wrote under the nom de plume 'Casque'.

The Bentley Boys at the 1927 Le Mans (previous page). Front row: Frank Clement, Leslie Callingham, Baron André d'Erlanger, George Duller, Sammy Davis, Dr John Dudley Benjafield. Both Captain Woolf 'Babe' Barnato and W.O. are standing behind.

In his encyclopaedic book on early Bentleys, Michael Hay names John Duff as the 'first of the "Bentley Boys"'[26], only to confuse matters by averring some pages later that 'In truth, Benjy [a bacteriologist called Dr J.D. Benjafield] was the first of the "Bentley Boys" that group of rich amateur sportsmen who were largely responsible for putting Bentleys on the map.'[27] As the former became associated with the marque in 1922 and the latter in 1924, both were certainly early devotees of the cars bearing the winged 'B', but it could be argued that the first of the Bentley Boys was actually the Westminster-educated son of a wealthy tea merchant.

Sidney Charles Houghton Davis was known to his friends as 'Sammy' and to his readers as 'Casque'. And he was busy 'putting Bentleys on the map' long before anyone, let alone a 'rich amateur', had even taken delivery of a Bentley.

Sammy is undoubtedly one of the most attractive characters of early motor racing. Modest and amusing, he was a talented author, artist and racing driver. Even though he worked for a living, he was a gentleman and embodied the chivalric spirit of the sport in its youth. Slightly older than many of the Bentley Boys, and eighteen months older than W.O., he was from the generation that had seen the birth of motoring in Great Britain.

Early opinion on the motorcar was, to say the least, divided. While there were some enthusiasts for the horseless carriage, the majority felt that it was simply a fad for rich dare-devils. Sammy was not rich, but he was a dare-devil, a romantic and a bit of a rebel, with a family background of unorthodox behaviour.

'He was discovered at the battle of Waterloo having a high old time when he should by rights have been on guard as duty officer at St James's Palace. He just went to Belgium because he couldn't miss the show', Sammy recalled of an antecedent who could well have been nineteenth-century dandy and diarist Captain Gronow.[28] One of his grandparents was a well-known artist who went to live among Native Americans, lost an eye while 'playing with cannon' and used to 'blow loudly on a coach horn from his studio window to attract beer from a neighbouring public house'. One of his grandmothers ran away 'with the other grandfather' and, to keep herself amused on a Sunday, used to read Wilkie Collins' novels that had been bound into her Bible. Sammy's mother 'adopted the bicycle at a time when such things were simply not done' and one of his sisters was so taken with a book she read about Tsarist Russia that she tried to make her way there equipped with four shillings and sixpence and a bag of bananas.[29]

Given such genes, it is hardly surprising that Sammy was so taken with the excitement of high-speed travel. He crashed a penny-farthing while at prep school, where one of his friends was an equally speed-obsessed lad called Malcolm Campbell.

Sammy was driving before W.O. was in his teens. 'My first drive in a car was in December 1900 when an uncle turned up with a 3½-h.p. Benz. It had the steering wheel in the middle and he allowed me to steer it for about a mile.'[30] At Westminster School his heroes were the great drivers of the turn of the century, who performed Herculean feats at such evocative events as the Paris–Vienna and the famously bloody Paris–Madrid race, which had to be stopped at

CHAPTER THREE

Modest and amusing, he was a talented author, artist and racing driver.

Sammy Davis standing by his car just before the start of the 1926 Le Mans.

Bordeaux by the French authorities because of the mounting death toll.

But it was the sense that motorists were a breed apart, outside the norm of late Victorian and Edwardian society, that appealed so much to young Sammy. 'Persecuted by the police, called evil names, assaulted if possible, the pioneers of motoring were a race without the law, untouchables, tinkers – people who were not – repeat not – gentlemen.'[31]

After Westminster he went to the Slade School of Art before becoming an apprentice at the Daimler Motor Works, and it was here that he got the nickname 'Sammy', given to him by one of the young typists. 'You see, an enthusiasm for machines was mixed with a total disregard for appearance, plus an inner feeling that oil was a necessary symbol of real "mechanic" status. Viewing the result with amused disfavour, my feminine critic produced a popular children's book called the "The Adventures of Little Black Sambo", alleging similarity, and the "Sambo" part stuck.'[32] Standards of what constituted racially offensive literature were very different in those distant days of the early twentieth century.

He left Daimler to pursue a career in journalism as an illustrator and writer. However, the nickname Sammy and the lack of concern about his appearance were to stay with him all his life, as was his fascination with motor vehicles. Since the persecuted brotherhood of pre-First World War motorists was small and select, it was inevitable that Sammy would come into contact with the Bentley brothers, who were making a name for themselves on motorcycles, as was Sammy, who recalled 'runs with H.M. Bentley on the carriers of Triumphs, long discussions with W.O. Bentley on the mysteries of Tourist Trophy racing, Rex or Indian'.[33]

With typical modesty, his memoirs play down his role in the Great War, but he served with distinction in the Royal Naval Auxiliary Service, a precursor to the Royal Electrical and Mechanical Engineers. Given his inclination towards internal combustion engines, it was appropriate that he served in the First Armoured Division of the British Army, driving armoured vehicles from trucks to Rolls-Royces. An excellent shot, he served as a sniper, shooting from a slow-moving car, and was gassed at Ypres, whereafter he served as an inspector of aero engines, which brought him back into contact with W.O. Eventually he had a breakdown, or as he put it, 'cracked up entirely and went to live in hospital'.[34]

In his own understated way he spoke for a generation when he wrote, 'after the war things were, somehow, very different. Like everyone else, I had lost too many friends to feel the same, among them were practically the whole of my family'.[35] However, in the world of the motorcar, he found some relief from the grief and guilt he felt about surviving the war when others had not been so lucky.

One who, like him, had lost those close to him but had himself survived the conflict, was W.O. Having shared experiences together during the war, it was natural that both men would continue to keep in touch after the Armistice. It seems that Sammy was something of a confidant of W.O.'s. 'I had, as it were, been behind the scenes while the Bentley grew, from an idea W.O. and I used to discuss almost daily'.[36] And in March 1919, barely two months after work had started on the 3-litre engine, *The Autocar*, for which Sammy worked, announced that development of 'A New British Sporting Car' was under way. A couple of months later there was another article, which went into more detail about the design, estimated price and accessories. On 29 November, after the explosive events in the mews that had brought life to the new marque, *The Autocar* championed the merits of the Bentley to its readers in a highly technical, in-depth, four-page article with drawings and diagrams under the headline 'A British Super-efficient Sporting Car, the Engine of which is Designed to keep its "tune" in the Hands of the Average Owner.'[37] In January 1920 Sammy took the new Bentley for a test drive.

Sammy Davis relaxing at Brooklands *(previous page) at the 1930 JCC Double 12 Hour Race.*

CHAPTER THREE

It was the Duke of Richmond and Gordon who described W.O. as 'a man "of few words". When they came they lacked nothing in force and finality!'³⁸ It is important to bear in mind W.O.'s taciturnity when reading his comment on Sammy's two-page article in *The Autocar*. He wrote in his autobiography:

> *The Autocar* published its first road test, a highly satisfactory one written in unmistakable style of 'Sammy' Davis. Besides the richly effective but not altogether relevant adjectives and classical analogies regarding 'speed' in general, the handling, the brakes, the comfort, and especially the sheer performance, were all highly praised, and the noise from the oil-pump drive was forgiven as a fault 'inseparable from the first chassis of a new design'. It stretched over two pages and there were three impressive photographs. How I wish we had had the cars we could have sold a dozen times over as a result of that piece of publicity!³⁹

From W.O. this was little short of remarkable, but then the piece that prompted this almost unqualified delight was a complete encomium. Typically Sammy took a pot shot at the authorities, and what he saw as the unreasonable persecution of the speed-seeking driver. A limit of 20 m.p.h. prevailed on British roads, so he gave the impression that the car had been tested at speed on private and French roads with the end of 'frustrating possible action by strait-laced, rigidly proper members of societies-for-the-prevention-of-everything'.⁴⁰ Having struck his blow for freedom on the roads, he turned to the vehicle, which performed 'with the air of a lithe, active, and speedy animal straining a little on the leash'.

Once Sammy let loose the beast, 'instantly the exhaust changed its note from a purr to a most menacing roar, the white ribbon of road streamed towards the car, while the backs of the seats pressed hard against one's shoulder blades'. But Sammy was far from done; as they topped seventy, the wind 'shrieked', and the surroundings became 'a blurred streak'. The speed and the roar of the exhaust combined to intoxicating effect: 'the pulse beats quicker, there comes an almost irresistible desire to burst into some

> **Once Sammy let loose the beast, 'instantly the exhaust changed its note from a purr to a most menacing roar.'**

wild war song, greater even than the immortal song of Roland' and there was plenty more in the same vein.⁴¹ The piece finished with the recommendation that for 'the man who wants a true sporting type of light bodied car for use on a Continental tour – where speed limits are not meant to be observed, unless one is involved in an accident – the 3-litre Bentley is undoubtedly the car *par excellence*'. In addition it also managed 'docility in traffic'. It would be wonderful indeed to see some of today's more serious and self-regarding motoring writers be moved by the urge to break into 'wild war song', and it would be interesting to see how many of them are familiar with the Chanson de Roland.

The war was over, the economy was booming and just 367 days after he and his fellow designers had had their first meeting, W.O. was reading a panegyric about his eponymous motorcar written by one of the leading motoring journalists of the day.⁴² Even the solitary and thoughtful Mr Bentley must have allowed himself a discreet grin of pleasure.

Chapter Four

By the late summer of 1921, the mood was rather

Bentley Motors factory works, from the earliest days at Cricklewood.

less optimistic

and *The Autocar* reported:

> Since the announcement in *The Autocar* of May 17th, 1919, that a Bentley car was to be produced, over two years have rolled by. Motorists to whom the chassis appealed especially have been wondering what was happening, why no cars succeeded the original experimental chassis, and, little by little, the rumour grew that the Bentley never would be a production job.[43]

The Bentley factory at Cricklewood, sadly this impressive building has long since been demolished.

After the initial excitement surrounding the new British sports car marque, there had been frustratingly little reason for customers to break into lusty war songs. Motor show visitors had seen a chassis, picked up a handsome brochure and … well … that was about it.

If not producing cars, the firm had nevertheless been busy, if a little surprised by the speed at which things had progressed. The factory, on recently acquired land at Cricklewood, was still being built when *The Autocar*'s glowing road test appeared. The company had also acquired a showroom, even if it had nothing to put in it. A.F.C. Hillstead, the sales manager, recalled:

> Bentley Motors showroom – number 3 Hanover Court – had been a dress shop, and much of the atmosphere of female fripperies remained when H.M. and I moved in. There were no offices; only two partitions shutting off a space that had been a trying-on room; no way of getting a car into the window, but a beautiful beige carpet. The company had no furniture to offer us, so we did the best we could with pieces from our respective homes. All we could muster in the way of sales' aids amounted to a framed photograph of our stand at Olympia; a watercolour of an imaginary Bentley at speed; some catalogues; a few reprints of the first descriptive article that appeared in *The Autocar*; one B.R. II cylinder mounted on a wooden base, and an abundant supply of optimism.[44]

There was something delightfully amateur about the whole set-up, characterised more by a cheerful have-a-go spirit of pluck and resourcefulness than by the detailed forecasts, sales projections, market research and business plans that would form part of a similar venture today. A sense of camaraderie prevailed, as Hillstead explained. 'We were all public-school men and, apart from speaking the same language, also possessed the same ideals; while our personal inclinations followed a similar pattern.'[45] Even the most exclusively educated of men might have been getting tired of waiting for his Bentley, but for at least one man the wait was over by the late summer of 1921.

One morning in September, a short, dapper young man turned up at the Bentley works. W.O. went out to meet him and walked with him to a 3-litre coupé. "Let us know if anything goes wrong, Noel", said W.O. "You've got a five-year guarantee, don't forget."[46] But the man was in no hurry to get away. Instead he cast a critical eye over the car, opened the bonnet and examined the engine carefully. At length he seemed satisfied and lowered the bonnet. Only then did he get into the driver's seat, start the engine and drive away. After watching the car disappear, W.O. turned and walked back to the factory where six more chassis were being finished. Production of the much-vaunted, 3-litre Bentley had begun and a rich young man-about-town called Noel Van Raalte had just become the very first customer of Bentley Motors.

While motoring had become more socially acceptable by the early 1920s, it remained a pastime of the social élite. As one teenage cockney mechanic who worked at Bentley Motors in the early days put it, revealingly, 'we didn't have a car in those days – no-one of our class could really afford to go motoring just yet'.[47]

The First World War may have come and gone, but Britain was still very much a class-bound society. Social and economic mobility were concepts of the future. Two-thirds of the nation's wealth was held by one per cent of the population. By the time Bentley sold his first car, the immediate post-war euphoria had waned, unemployment was around one million; and if he could find work, a manual labourer would be lucky to earn more than four pounds a week. The 3-litre Bentley, on the other hand, in which Van Raalte had driven away from the Bentley factory, had cost £1,050 for the chassis alone; bodywork was at least £200 or £300 extra.[48] The total cost was about as much as a working man made, gross, in three or four years.

Bentley exploited the socio-economic situation. The way he saw it, Bentley Motors was a sort of invitation-only club, the price of membership being the cost of a Bentley. Being a public-school man, W.O. knew money alone should not guarantee membership. Bentley was not just aiming his car at the top one per cent of the population; he wanted to select his customers himself, weed out the cads, the bounders, those who were not sportsmen and, above all, those who did not understand a beautiful piece of machinery like his 3-litre engine. He wasn't asking for much; he was just concerned that his 'choice' (Bentley's word) of first owner sent out the right messages:

> He would naturally be sympathetic to the sort of car we were producing or he wouldn't be paying over £1,000 for his model. But he also had to be something of a social butterfly who would mix in the best social strata and spread the good word far and wide, and something of an engineer who could appreciate the qualities of his car, talk about them authoritatively, and come back to explain any snags to us.[49]

Happily Van Raalte was the perfect choice: '[He] was very rich. He owned Brownsea Island, among other properties, and put up the money for K.L.G. plugs. He was very sociable.'[50] Rich, a Society figure and possessed of 'excellent mechanical knowledge'[51], Van Raalte was also a sportsman. As an undergraduate at Cambridge he had endeared himself to college authorities and fellow road users alike by racing a Grand Prix Mercedes around the streets of the fenland town in reverse gear. Typical of the Van Raalte style was a race one Sunday morning to the station, starting at the Market Square; he pitted his 140-h.p. Minerva against a friend's Grand Prix Fiat and won: his prize was that the loser paid the fines.

The choice of Van Raalte as a 'brand ambassador' was a shrewd one, as Bentley's sales manager Hillstead pointed out. 'This was an extremely wise move, as not only was he a friend of W.O.'s but also a clever engineer and could be relied upon to inform us of any of those small troubles which are apt to crop up during the early stages of the life of a new model.'[52]

W.O.'s faith in Van Raalte as a proselytiser of the marque was not misplaced. Within days of collecting his

The Cricklewood factory interior, showing the production line in 1921.

new car, Van Raalte had struck up a lively correspondence with the motoring press. 'The reason I bought a Bentley was because of its exceptional performance in all respects on the road', wrote Van Raalte to the Editor of *The Autocar* on 1 October 1921. However this was but a prelude to the sort of encomium that eclipses even the firm's most grandiose advertisements of later years. 'Such features as steering, suspension, holding the road, brakes, change speed, and engine efficiency, leave nothing to be desired, and are, in my opinion, to be found to a higher degree in this make of car than any other of the many makes I have owned or used. I dislike drawing comparison', but manfully he overcame his aversion to compare the Bentley favourably to what many had hitherto regarded as the best car in the world: 'I admire the Rolls-Royce intensely, and have owned two of them, and must say that, as regards the features I have mentioned, the Bentley is far in advance of it, while the price is £750 less.'

Given that it was only two years earlier that first Bentley engine had spluttered to life, one could be forgiven for thinking that Van Raalte was a major shareholder, keen to see his investment pay off. However, he was quick to reassure the readers of *The Autocar*'s correspondence page that this was far from being the case. 'I have no interest in the company beyond owning and appreciating one of their cars.'[53]

And appreciate them he did. Almost as soon as he got his first Bentley, Van Raalte was making modifications and improvements, either at the machine shop that he had at his house near Southampton or at the Bentley factory. As one of Bentley's mechanics recalled, 'there was always a lot to do to that car, refinements he wanted: undershields to be made, streamlining for the back and front axle.'[54] It was also his idea that every Bentley should carry an extra half set

Bentley Motors was a sort of invitation-only club, the price of membership being the cost of a Bentley.

Noel Van Raalte, Bentley's first customer.

of spark plugs, which, as he was a director of K.L.G., was a shrewd suggestion. The mechanic continued:

> He was a fine driver, and he was the man who had a yacht maroon [flare gun] fitted at the side of the car because he got so fed up with trying to get past lorries. He used to fire this thing, and the lorry driver would immediately put everything on and pull over, thinking a back tyre had gone. He was a great character van [sic] Raalte, and he thought the world of the Bentley. He knew his stuff, too – a real good judge of a motor-car.[55]

Van Raalte was a loyal and enthusiastic Bentley customer, with a sporting nature: he kept up the racing interest that he had developed at Cambridge, and later drove in the Indianapolis 500 race. He was always interested in what was coming next from the Cricklewood works and so it was natural that when W.O. came out with a 100-m.p.h. version of the 3-litre he would take delivery of the first of those too.

Van Raalte's frequent visits to the works and reciprocal trips by Bentley staff to his home meant he struck up a rapport with the engineering and sales staff in addition to his friendship with W.O. Hillstead recalls with fondness the invitations to Van Raalte's house on the River Hamble in Hampshire. 'He was a true friend, though just a little eccentric'.[56] His love of cars was in no doubt; he even brought them into his house: 'he had converted his drawing-room into an extremely well-equipped machine-shop complete with a universal grinder'.[57]

He may have loved his Bentleys so much that he had them live under the same roof, but this did not exclude other interests too. He had several powerboats and had fitted a tank engine into an ex-naval vessel to serve as a motor yacht.

Although Noel Van Raalte did not really figure as a Bentley Boy in the popular imagination, he was most certainly in that mould. With Van Raalte as an owner, W.O. had pulled off a major P.R. coup, but Van Raalte was just one component in a cleverly put together public relations machine. Road tests were all very well, but the Bentley would drive to fame on the racetrack.

CHAPTER FIVE

What was so

lovely was the original Brooklands committee',

Sammy Davis fondly recalled many years later when he was well into his eighties:

> They had all come from horse-racing, and with the exception of Jarrott and Montagu's father – he wasn't Lord Montagu then – they didn't know the first thing about it, and they proceeded, you would hardly believe it, they proceeded to insist that everybody should wear a coloured shirt and cap, exactly like a jockey, and they treated the drivers just like jockeys, they weren't even allowed in the club house bar.[58]

By the early 1920s Brooklands was open again for competitive motoring, and a thrill-hungry cadre of daredevil drivers was keen to pit their machines against each other and the record books.

CHAPTER FIVE

Bank Holiday meeting at Brooklands, August 1928 (previous page). The crowds enjoy a picnic while the cars line up in front of the Vickers sheds.

The 1926 RAC English Grand Prix; the first Grand Prix held on British soil took place at Brooklands on 7 August 1926.

Brooklands held its inaugural meeting on 6 July 1907 and motor racing, which was already a part of life on the Continent, the Isle of Man and in Ireland, arrived in Edwardian England. With its racetrack and airstrip, Brooklands was, in effect, society's concession to the new-fangled flying machines and horseless carriages: a place close to London where the affluent aviator could indulge his passion for flying and the moneyed motorist test his machine flat out on the Railway straight and show his skill on the impressive 'wall-of-death'-style banking. Habitués of the early Brooklands spoke of its first decade with lyricism: 'the absence of advertisements, no disfiguring bridge over the finishing straight, and Mrs Billing's Blue Bird Café housed in one of the hangars'.[59]

However, the site was turned over to military use during the First World War. In 1917 the Blue Bird burnt down and at the end of the war it took a couple of years to repair the damage done to the road surface by the solid-wheeled trucks used by the armed forces. But by the early 1920s Brooklands was open again for competitive motoring, and a thrill-hungry cadre of daredevil drivers was keen to pit their machines against each other and the record books. The Junior Car Club's 200 Mile race at Brooklands in 1921 was the first big post-war race in England.

During 1920 a short, stocky, softly spoken man, his shock of hair parted neatly in the middle, joined the company to replace Gallop, who had gone to work for the noted racing driver Count Zborowski. Reserved in company, Frank Clement was anything but reticent on the racetrack; a prominent racing driver before the war, he was also a talented development engineer and was the perfect man to head up the experimental department. In 1921 a 3-litre experimental Bentley, EXP2, was entered into the short handicap organised by the Essex Motor Club for cars with an engine capacity of over 1700c.c. Clement was to drive. The decision was a bold one as delivery of the first model was still some time off, but W.O. must have decided almost as soon as he had got a working car that it would

THE BEGINNINGS OF BENTLEY

Frank Clement at the 1923 Le Mans. He was to race for Bentley in every Le Mans they contested up until 1930.

have to prove itself racing for the marque to stand any chance of building a reputation among the all-important, dogmatic motor-racing fraternity.

The Bentley started promisingly but finished on three cylinders. The comment of a journalist from *The Motor*, that 'The Bentley seemed a certain winner', was of little consolation to W.O., who as ever had little to say but wore a revealingly grim expression. The race was won by someone called Lionel Martin driving a car of his own design, which he called an Aston Martin.[60]

Downcast but undeterred, W.O. entered EXP2 for the Brooklands Whitsun Meeting. It was again unplaced in its first race, but 'ran well, covering the half-mile at about 95 m.p.h.'[61], passing Woolf Barnato, a rich young man at the wheel of an American Locomobile with an engine of over eight litres. The second race that EXP2 entered was a sprint ... and it won. *The Motor* recorded this historic moment of Bentley's first victory in competitive motoring: 'starting from scratch the Bentley got away cleanly, accelerated like a hare and won by a comfortable margin'.[62]

It was not a remarkable victory, but it was enough to get Bentley talked about and to inspire W.O. to enter the 1922 Isle of Man T.T. with a team of three cars. While the track cars were in preparation, A.F.C. Hillstead, Bentley's highly effective salesman in the early years of the firm, asked for the showroom demonstrator to be fitted with a racing body. Its appearance must have caused quite a stir on the sedate streets of Mayfair. 'The body itself, being of aluminium, was scratched over with a wire brush and varnished, which had the effect of giving a white finish with a slight tendency towards iridescence, and the wings, frame and upholstery were of pillar-box red', recorded the sales manager, adding with commendable understatement, 'This combination may sound a trifle vulgar to the modern motorist, but it never failed to attract attention.'[63] With cars in production, a growing racing reputation and the exotic, eye-catching two-seater making test runs, the future seemed promising.

Just as the car was different, so too was the way in which it was sold, as Hillstead recalled. This was no straightforward matter of making a quick test run, choosing some bodywork and signing a contract. The Bentley customer was as unusual and intriguing as the vehicle he was buying. Almost every buyer became a personal friend. Sales followed a pattern: a technical chat about the engine, some social banter, a brisk test run with some fancy gear changes by Hillstead, a look round the engine assembly shop, a thrilling run of up to 80 m.p.h. along the North Circular and then, of course, lunch where, 'under the mellowing influence of alcohol, the real business was tackled'.[64]

Moreover it seemed that W.O.'s vision of Bentley Motors as a fraternity of like-minded sportsmen was taking shape. People were not buying a car, they were joining a club, taking on a new interest; in general the customers

CHAPTER FIVE

were keen to become part of the Bentley Motors story – they were 'living the brand'. 'Apart from the fact that [the customer] was spending well over one thousand pounds he invariably seemed to take an interest in the affairs of the Company. What was our racing programme? Was W.O. going to design another aero engine? How was the financial situation? were just a few of the questions asked.'[65]

'How was the financial situation?' A simple enough question, but a sensitive one. Even though the company was not yet three years old, its finances were parlous. Hillstead wrote two books about his experience in the motor trade. The first, *Those Bentley Days*, was a more-or-less cheerful account of those years. The second, *Fifty Years With Motor Cars*, was much more bitter and resentful, revealing divisions between the sales and engineering sides of the business. In particular, the second book shows that his relationship with W.O. was a strained one; by contrast Hillstead got on well with H.M.

There is little doubt that as a salesman he felt, or was made to feel, inferior. His second book is constantly littered with interpolations and asides, along the lines of 'well, I was only a sales bloke'.[66] Personal disposition aside, it would seem that part of the reason for Hillstead's dissatisfaction lay in the uncertain financial basis of the firm, in which he was a small investor. According to Hillstead, while the public façade may have been one of racing victory and smart sporting customers who flowed through life on a tide of Champagne, the financial background to Bentley Motors was very much a hand-to-mouth business, right from the very beginning.

W.O. Bentley on one of the few occasions he drove competitively for Bentley, competing in the 1922 Isle of Man TT.

> The Bentley customer was as unusual and intriguing as the vehicle he was buying.

Hillstead regularly made the rounds of potential investors and each missed sale had the potential to sink the young company: an immense responsibility. He recalls one sale that typified the underlying uncertainty:

> On one occasion, when the prospect was indeed gloomy, I had a chance of obtaining an order for six chassis from a London coachbuilder. H.M. was aware of this and, as there happened to be a board meeting which coincided with my appointment, if I were successful then I was to let him know so that the good news could be broadcast. I was successful to the extent of obtaining a substantial deposit cheque, and this I sent to H.M., thus enabling him to secure yet a further period of grace.[67]

Additional pressure came from what Hillstead saw as H.M.'s fraternal instinct to shield his younger brother as far as possible from the depressing financial realities of being in the car business in the 1920s: 'I know something of the way H.M. battled in the early days to keep W.O. as free from financial problems as the circumstances permitted.'[68] There was the sense that much was done to keep the austere W.O. happy, at least as happy as he could be, allowing him to immerse himself in his engineering and design work.

It is with these factors in mind that one should interpret Hillstead's remark in *Those Bentley Days*:

> It seemed that we were quite unique in the motor world. The Bentley was being discussed in the highest engineering circles and, amongst the buying public, it was already considered to be enjoying the same degree of excellence and popularity as the Rolls-Royce. How had this been achieved in such a short time? We had no idea, except that the car was good and the only one of its kind in existence.[69]

W.O. at the wheel of his 1922 3-litre T.T. car, next to him is riding mechanic Leslie Pennal.

O. BENTLEY.
T.T. RACE. 1922.

CHAPTER SIX
Some measure of W.O.'s enthusiasm

for his cars to compete (as well as his ignorance of, or indifference to, the firm's finances) was to be seen in the decision to enter a Bentley in the Indianapolis 500 Mile race in May 1922.

> W.O. had gambled on the natural British instinct of championing the underdog and it paid off handsomely.

The car had no chance of winning, but it averaged roughly 80 m.p.h. There was no distribution for the marque in the U.S. and it seems a strange, albeit sporting, action on W.O.'s part.

One month later, more explicable was the decision to enter a Bentley works team into the Isle of Man T.T., which was being run for the first time since 1914. The excitement was intense. It should be remembered that with few motor-racing circuits in the modern sense, competitive motor sport was usually run on public road circuits. One of the better known of these was the 37¾-mile circuit on the Isle of Man.

Given such a long circuit over public roads, it was difficult for a driver to acquaint himself with every undulation and turn, and calculate the perfect angle for entering each corner. The Bentley team drove the cars it was to compete in to Liverpool and boarded the ferry for the Isle of Man. While the other teams had built their cars especially for the race, W.O. was keen to stress his cars were unmodified – genuine touring models – and went as far as to issue an uncompromising statement to the effect: 'We would like to point out that, unlike our competitors, we have not built special racing cars for this event, but instead entered three standard chassis drawn from our production stock.'[70] A photograph of the Bentley team shows a proud W.O. standing in the middle of a row of smartly turned-out works drivers in white overalls embroidered with the winged 'B' motif. This time W.O. himself was among the drivers; as the race was about to begin he walked to his saloon car, took something out and then returned to the racing car. Lifting up the seat cushion he stowed a bandage and a small bottle of brandy underneath … just in case.

Run in abominable weather, the race, in the words of one account, 'deteriorated into little more than a high speed reliability trial'.[71] Clement, the works driver who had entered the last T.T. in 1914 for Straker-Squire, acquitted himself well, managing second place to the Sunbeam of Chassagne, while W.O. was narrowly pushed into fourth place by a Vauxhall, with a margin of six seconds. Hawkes, the only professional driver in the team, came fifth, despite losing a plug and all his water early on.

The race had achieved W.O.'s aim of putting 'the cars in the public eye' and making them a talking point: despite a somewhat sparse entry, the T.T. attracted major racing talent, including Segrave, the famous French driver Chassagne, 'Bill' Guinness and a host of others, including 'the Marquis of Casa Maury, an international sportsman, a dark dashing gentleman of pleasure and business, of Colombian origin', who drove a Bugatti to third place in a race for small cars that was run simultaneously.[72]

Press coverage was spectacular, revelling in the fact that the Bentley team, driving cars that were pretty nearly standard models, had held up so well in the face of competition from specially prepared racing cars. W.O. had gambled on the natural British instinct of championing the underdog and it had paid off handsomely. Typical of the reports of the event was a piece in the *Sunday Times* of 25 June:

> The most outstanding feature of the race was the running of the Bentleys. The only complete team to finish, and occupying second, fourth and fifth positions, their unquestionable claim to glory is based on the fact that, for all practical purposes, they were standard stock cars as sold to the general public.[73]

The reaction was instantaneous. As the Bentleys crossed the finishing line, a man called out to the Bentley pits, "I'm George Porter of Blackpool, and I want the agency for Lancashire. The car of yours is going to be a world-beater."[74] Porter went on to become a devoted and energetic agent for the marque. A new regional representative was not all that W.O. came away with.

Travelling back to the mainland, W.O. got talking on the boat to an extrovert man brimming with bonhomie and instantly identified by his unforgettable 'deep throaty "belly-laugh"'.[75] Herbert 'Bertie' Kensington Moir had competed in the race at the wheel of an Aston Martin. His fondness for the good life was obvious; lean as a youth, he was beginning to fill out and

W.O. careering round a bend in his only competitive race for Bentley, the 1922 Isle of Man T.T.

The 1922 T.T. crew: Hawkes, Clement, and W.O. with mechanics Pennal, Browning and Saunders.

Hawkes and Browning in the Indianapolis 3-litre, the Bentley team's first international race.

would later become decidedly portly. Bertie was able to bring the normally reticent W.O. out of himself. The two men hit it off right away: 'we talked clear across the Irish Sea, through the night and through quite a few more drinks'.[76] At dawn on the dockside at Liverpool, W.O. asked his amusing drinking companion if would like to come and join Bentley Motors. "I think that would be a very good idea" came the response from a clearly delighted Bertie.[77]

Sporting significance aside, the race is interesting in that it marked the start of the myth of the hard-partying Bentley Boys. The mechanics lost no time picking up local girls. "We went to a dance and met some girls, and had a real whale of a time, and", as these things have a habit of doing, "it got to the early hours of the morning".[78] Locked out of the hotel, an attempt to get back into their rooms by climbing a rope of knotted blankets ended with them sprawled on the pavement crying with laughter, their best suits somewhat the worse for wear. By now they were in no state for anything; dawn was coming fast and with it the early morning practice run, so instead they scaled the gate into the yard where the cars were kept, the noise waking W.O.'s dog.

So that started W.O.'s little dog barking; he always has his little Peke[79] with him, and it lived in his car. Luckily nobody came, and we got in to the yard and into the car. 'Course the dog yapped harder than ever then. We kept saying, "Shut up, you little b____," and Bert kept saying, "Give him a thump." "No," I said, "don't – leave him alone, he's all right." Any rate, we finally quietened this damn dog down after about ten minutes, and we managed to get some sort of sleep in the back of the car.[80]

Such antics came to characterise the behaviour of the Bentley mechanics at more or less every race. As their pit work improved in speed and efficiency so did their appetite for the pleasures of life away from home.

We used to see the other racing stables working all night, and we'd say, 'They're still learning – they haven't got down to it yet like we have'. They'd perhaps be ten days over there before the race and never get a night out at all. We used to pull their legs and feel so sorry for them. 'Come and have a beer,' we'd say. 'Let's go and make whoppee.' But they never could.

All the same, us Bentley boys were really well liked – with all the other boys, teams, and that – we really were. And we were always called the 'Bentley Boys' by the others. It didn't dawn on us for ages that the drivers were being called the Bentley Boys as well; I think it was the papers that started that. We had called ourselves that for so long, right from the beinning, that we just thought of ourselves as the Bentley Boys – and we were proud of it – it was something to be proud of.[81]

> 'We just thought of ourselves as the Bentley Boys – and we were proud of it – it was something to be proud of.'

Clement's 3 Litre speeding along the Isle of Man T.T. course.

CHAPTER SEVEN

a couple of months after the newsworthy, profile-building T.T., Bentley racked up another competitive honour, which, in the story of the Bentley Boys, was even more significant than the team's exploits on the Isle of Man.

THE BEGINNINGS OF BENTLEY

> To the mechanics and engineers Duff was simply 'Tons of guts'.

Frank Clement in his Bentley chases Joyce in a diminutive A.C. (previous page) during a race at Brooklands on Easter Monday, April 1923.

John Duff in an unidentified car, preparing to compete in the 1926 500 Mile race in Indianapolis.

Over two days in September, a 3-litre Bentley, once again a more-or-less standard car with a four-seater body, took the Double Twelve Hours record at Brooklands, travelling 2,083 miles at an average speed of 86.79 m.p.h.

Mere statistics alone do not convey the near-Herculean nature of this achievement. The Brooklands Double Twelve was demanding. Because night-time racing at Brooklands was not allowed, a 24-hour trial had to be held over two consecutive days. It must be remembered that considerable physical strength was needed to drive cars of that era at speed for 12 hours at a stretch. Moreover, the banking at Brooklands had no retaining wall and, while it had been adequate for motor vehicles of the Edwardian world, the sports and racing cars of the 1920s were possessed of such power as to require considerable driver strength to stop them going over the top and, in all likelihood, killing the driver outright.

John Duff was the man who took the record, driving a privately owned Bentley. One young visitor to the paddock at Brooklands described him as 'very tall and lanky with a long face [who] often wore plus-fours'.[82] Photographs show exactly such a man. There is one particularly famous image that shows Duff in his Bentley days: arranged in ascending height from left to right are Clement, W.O. and Duff. There is something of the adventurer about Duff. Feet wide apart, hands planted defiantly on his hips, his sporty plus-fours teamed with a thick roll-neck sweater and tweed jacket, his jaw set with determination, goggles on his forehead keeping the thick dark hair out of his eyes – there is no doubt that he was an imposing figure.

It is an understatement to say that by the time he competed in the Double Twelve that autumn, 27-year-old Duff had led an incident-packed life. Born in Kiukiang in China in January 1895, Duff was congenitally unsuited to life as the son of missionary parents. As a youngster he learned to ride wild horses and shoot wild boar. Packing him off to an aunt in Canada only served to add poker player and cowhand to his growing repertoire of non-ecclesiastical skills. He was back in China when the First World War broke out and boarded the Trans-Siberian express making for England. Anyone who has read Solzhenitsyn's *August 1914* knows what a confused state Russia was in, suffering huge losses on the front with Germany. Nevertheless Duff made it to England, where the recruiting office at first, perhaps unsurprisingly, took a sceptical view of his story. He joined the Royal Berkshire Rifles and was promoted to Captain. Like so many officers of the time, he was used to leading from the front – so much in front that he was hit by friendly fire and invalided back to England. Even the understated W.O. described Duff as 'a man with tremendous guts and determination'.[83] To the mechanics and engineers Duff was simply 'Tons of guts'.[84]

Looking around for excitement after the war he found a 10-litre Fiat, capable of topping 100 m.p.h. After that he purchased another Fiat to wrestle with, a monstrous black vehicle known as Mephistopheles. Even

then, the brute power of this car was insufficient for him, and in an effort to raise the compression ratio; he caused the engine to explode in a race. Duff is said to have sold the remains of the second Fiat to an enthusiast who fitted it with 21.7-litre Fiat airship engine, using it to take the land speed record in 1924.[85]

Finished with Fiats, Duff moved on to Bentleys. Already a dealer, trading under the name 'Sporting Cars Ltd.', he was offered the agency for Bentley provided he could find a partner with centrally located and well-equipped premises. He met fellow motor trader William Adlington at Brooklands and the two men subsequently went into business together at 10 Upper St Martin's Lane in Central London as 'Duff and Adlington'.

Having done some work on the engine of his Bentley himself and removed the wings, Duff appeared at Brooklands. Walter Hassan, one of the mechanics assigned to him by Bentley, takes up the story.

> Duff really was tough. In that 'Double Twelve' record he drove single-handed with no stuffing in the seat – a steel bucket seat. And after the first twelve hours he more or less had to be lifted out of the car, and practically carried up to the Hand and Spear in Weybridge, where we all stayed. It didn't really seem to us that he could carry on the next day. But he never questioned it, and, of course, he did carry on. It was his own idea to have no stuffing in the seat: he was a man of many ideas, very thorough and keen, Duff was.[86]

However the Spartan seating was a major problem. 'His back was absolutely raw', another mechanic recalled, seeing Duff after the first round of racing.

> The trouble was that he'd got the peak of the seat just under the shoulder-blades. He'd had it made himself, and thought it was fine – but he'd forgotten he had to do twenty-four grinding hours in that seat. That was unlike Duff; he usually thought out everything very well in advance. I remember we helped him into the bath and then straight to bed that night, but he was so tough that he was as right as rain in the morning.[87]

'Right as rain' is something of an overstatement – at one pit stop early in the afternoon of the second day, Duff jumped out of the car desperate to empty his bladder behind a shed. Time passed and with the car refuelled, but Duff nowhere to be see, and with W.O.'s eyes boring into the pit staff, one of the mechanics ran behind the shed where Duff said that he been unable to perform the necessary adjustments to his clothing as his fingers were so numb.

However, as soon as he could, he was back in training for the following year's motor racing: Duff really did believe in meticulous preparation, both mechanical and physical; putting himself through a regime of bracing swims in the lake on Hampstead Heath and runs of at least twenty miles a week.[88] Indeed his approach to training was surprisingly modern; he was

John Duff in a Bentley (above) at a race meet at Brooklands.

Clement, W.O. and Duff (opposite) with the 1924 Le Mans winning 3-litre Bentley.

CHAPTER SEVEN

particularly careful to monitor his diet. One of the race mechanics recalled how he was to be seen…

> with a huge sheet tied up like a navvy's handkerchief, full of fresh lettuce, a whole bag of fresh eggs, and a jar of honey. This peculiar diet of his was always a great joke with us boys, and he used to lecture us how wrong it was the way we ate huge quantities of meat and all that sort of thing. There was nothing like pure food, he'd say. It was one of the most amusing sights to see him, after a spell of driving, sitting behind the pits with a spoon: he'd take a spoonful of neat honey and put it in his mouth; he'd crack an egg and swallow that, and then he'd take leaves of lettuce.[89]

Duff was obviously preparing for something big, but when he announced what he wanted to do with a Bentley, he took everybody by complete surprise. He called into Bentley's sales office on Hanover Street and casually announced that a race was being planned in France that would run for 24 hours non-stop. He then mentioned that he was going to enter and that he wanted Bentley to support him: preparing the car, supplying mechanical backup and giving him a co-driver. The race was to be held near a small town called Le Mans.

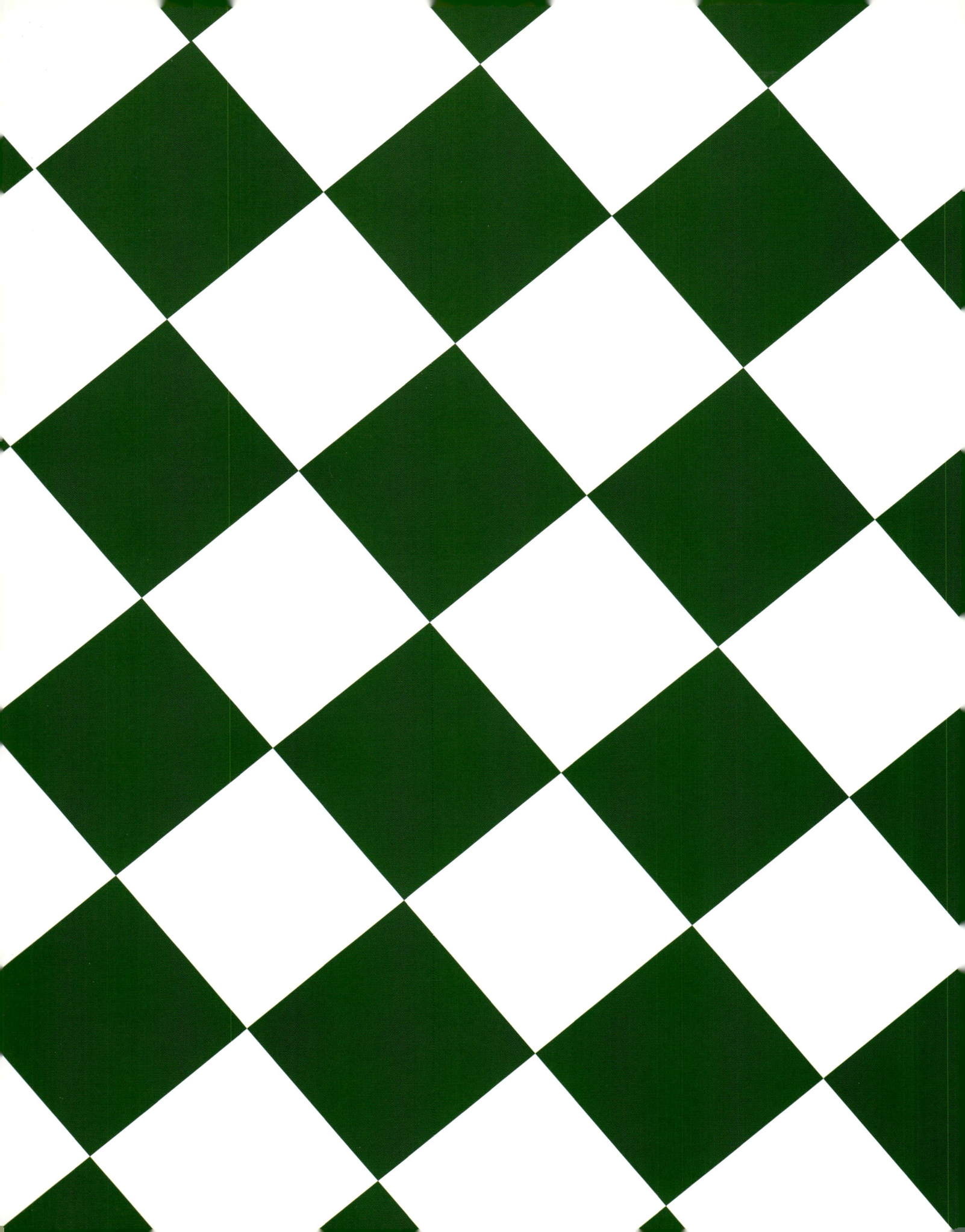

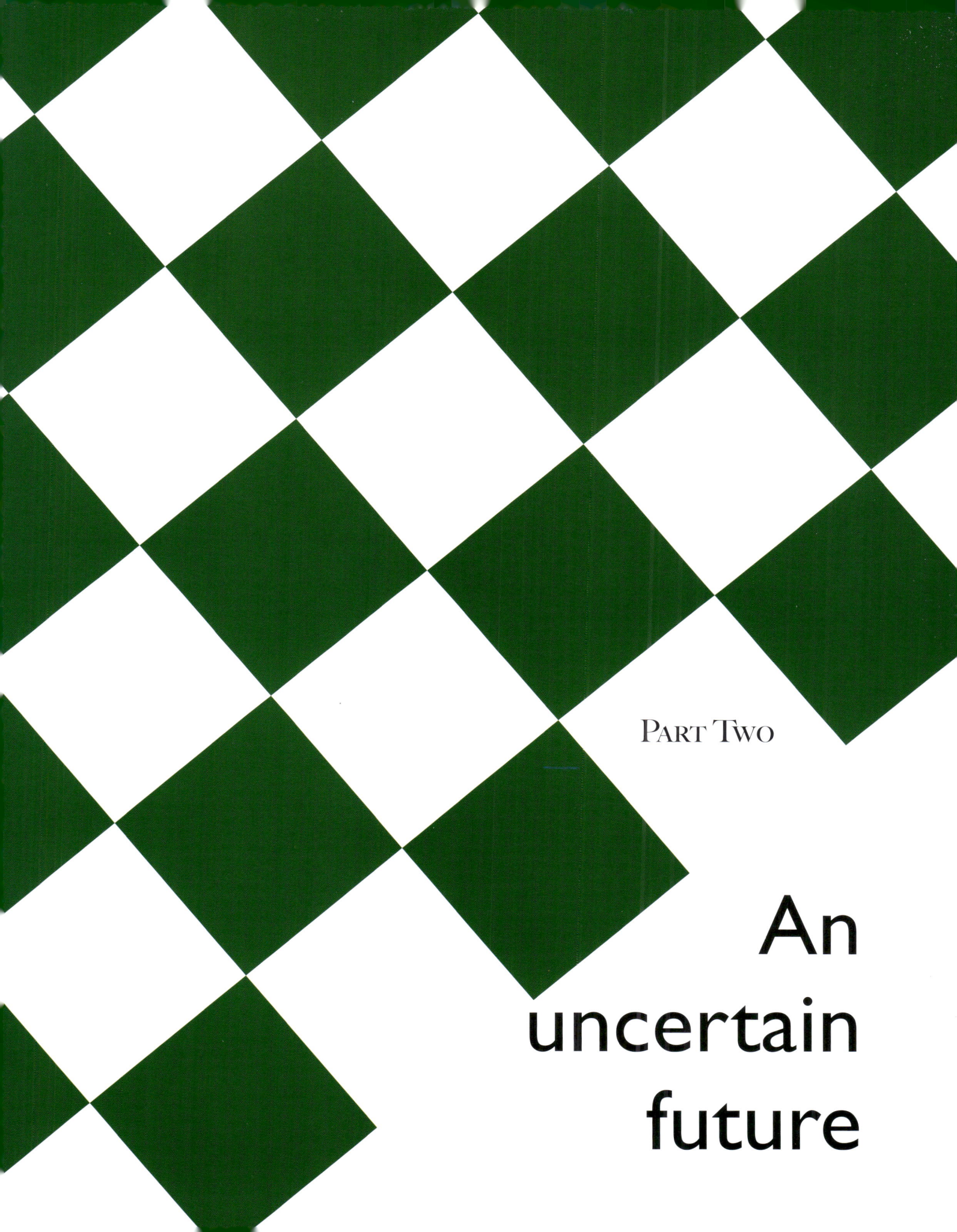

Part Two

An uncertain future

CHAPTER EIGHT

i think the whole

thing's crazy",

exploded W.O. Bentley in a rare moment of passion. "Nobody'll finish. Cars aren't designed to stand that sort of strain for twenty-four hours."[9]

> W.O. was, at first, implacably opposed to the race that, in a few years, would deliver his marque lasting fame and immortality.

It is strange to think, looking back, that W.O. was, at first, implacably opposed to the race that, in a few years, would deliver his marque lasting fame and immortality. However, Bentley's objection was simple enough to understand. Nobody had ever tried anything like this before. Racing for long periods around a specially prepared motor-racing circuit was one thing; conducting a race and reliability trial over country roads, some of them little more than rutted cart tracks, in the middle of France for 24 hours without ceasing, was another thing altogether. Having gained excellent publicity for the reliability of his cars – dependability, as well as speed, was one of W.O.'s cherished goals – why should he risk the good name of his company in a race that was to be run under conditions so demanding that no other British manufacturer was even entering a car?

Duff was a forceful and persuasive character, however, and eventually W.O. relented, consenting to

CHAPTER EIGHT

The 1923 Le Mans gets under way (previous page); despite W.O.'s initial scorn it was the first of eight successive Le Mans that Bentley were to compete in.

Duff and Clement's Bentley, the only British entrant at 1923 Le Mans, at speed on the rutted course.

AN UNCERTAIN FUTURE

"Come on", he announced, "We've got to go and see this stupid race. We'll take the night boat."

Duff and Clement, with their 1923 Le Mans car.

Duff's requests. The Experimental Department would prepare the car under Clement's guidance, while Clement himself was detailed as co-driver with two mechanics as pit crew.

The journey on the long dusty roads of France in early summer 1923 was, in the words of Clement, "extraordinarily light-hearted and casual".[91] Duff and Clement simply piled everything into the car that they would be driving in the race, loaded the mechanics into the back seat and drove off as if setting out on a continental motoring tour.

While Clement was driving down from Dieppe, W.O. was assailed by second thoughts concerning the whole Le Mans adventure. A thorough man, it must have galled him to think that he would not be there to oversee the final preparations and monitor the performance of the car during the race. Moreover, it must have occurred to him that, whether he was there or not, he would be answerable for the performance of the car that bore his name. Besides, he was beginning to be mildly curious about the race. In 1923, as today, the race was scheduled to start at four o'clock on Saturday afternoon, and by the Friday morning W.O. was 'in a fever of anxiety and suffering from a very bad conscience'.[92] After lunch he could not stand it any longer and drove from the Cricklewood works to Hanover Street, where he found Hillstead. "Come on", he announced, "We've got to go and see this stupid race. We'll take the night boat."[93]

As soon as they crossed the Channel, W.O. clammed up, his usual shyness compounded doubtless by his anxiety at the coming race and a disinclination to try to speak French. When Hillstead complained, he was 'treated to a flow of invective that put a stop to any interchange of opinions for some considerable time'.[94] The weather was sultry and almost unbearably hot; neither man had had time to purchase refreshments and, by the time their train was halfway to Le Mans, they were parched. "Never again", vowed W.O. "Next time we bring the car."[95]

When he arrived, Bentley took over the running of the pits and dispatched Hillstead to a heap of sand up the road from the pits to act as timekeeper. Having got

CHAPTER EIGHT

things arranged the way he liked them, he settled down to watch the race and found himself ineluctably drawn to it. His doubts evaporated with every passing lap and within a few hours he was hooked. 'Before darkness fell and the acetylene arc lamps at the corners were turned on, Le Mans was beginning to get into my blood. By midnight, with the cars pounding past the stand with their lights on – my first sight of racing in the dark – I was quite certain that this was the best race I had ever seen.' Bentley had realised that Le Mans fitted his cars perfectly. 'The rugged course with long straights exactly suited the Bentley.'[96]

The weather had broken: almost the instant the starter's flag fell, a hailstorm began, followed by heavy rain lasting four hours and transforming the rough track, village streets and rutted country road into a sodden morass. Mud and water were blinding the drivers of faster cars (particularly nasty as neither Duff nor Clement drove with goggles or, indeed, any kind of headgear), while the drivers of slower cars found themselves engulfed in a wave of muck every time they were overtaken. Yet, out of this automotive mud-wrestling match, the Bentley emerged, to the surprise of the French crowd, in a strong position. The demanding conditions took their toll on the vehicles, and a stray stone, kicked up at dusk, cost the Bentley one of its lights, but it otherwise proved itself more than equal to the punishing course, establishing several lap records until around noon on the Sunday, when another stone holed the petrol tank and brought it to a standstill.

Duff, who was at the wheel when the car died and rolled to a halt, ran the three miles from the stranded car to the pits. Immediately, Clement set off on a bicycle borrowed (without the owner's knowledge) from a French soldier, to the ironic cheers of the crowd, a couple of petrol cans slung over his shoulder. He nursed the car to the pits with the cycle in the back. The hole was repaired and the car went on to record the fastest lap of the race and, although the petrol tank débâcle had cost two and a half hours, managed to finish fourth. *The Autocar*, which reported on the event, was thrilled by the Bentley's performance

Immediately, Clement set off on a bicycle borrowed from a French soldier.

and even W.O. managed a flicker of emotion. 'I was never more surprised and delighted than when we came in fourth in that first somewhat casual and slap-happy effort.'[97]

Looking at photographs from the first Le Mans, the overwhelming impression is of cars tearing around a part of rural France little changed since the time Balzac was writing his novels of French provincial life. Yet the first signs of the unique Le Mans experience were detectable: a jazz band played non-stop at the American bar; loudspeakers relayed a concert direct from the Eiffel Tower; the night sky exploded into vivid colour with a firework display an hour before midnight; an open-air cinema was in operation. And there was a restaurant, sponsored by a manufacturer of shock absorbers, into which wet, muddy drivers were hauled for 'hot onion soup' and 'plates of roast chicken', after which they 'were called upon to assist in emptying innumerable bottles of champagne'. The drivers acquitted themselves nobly at the dinner table, dispatching 'fifty chickens, 150 gallons of hot soup, 450 bottles of champagne, and unknown quantities of red and white wine'.[98]

The Le Mans legend had started and Bentley was already an integral part of it.

Chapter Nine

The remainder of 1923 was not particularly memorable

Dr Benjafield + the Bentley

in terms of racing results. Later that summer the indomitable Duff entered the Touring Grand Prix of Guipuscoa at the Lasarte circuit near San Sebastian in northern Spain. He took the lead in lap five and held it for eight laps until a flying stone shattered his goggles, causing him to lose control and crash.

AN UNCERTAIN FUTURE

> Style and sporting attitude counted for more than rules and regulations.

This was, however, a time when style and sporting attitude counted for more than rules and regulations, and as the judges were so impressed with Duff's panache and a terrific run with an average speed of 65 m.p.h. (almost 10 m.p.h. faster than the eventual winner's average) they decided to award him the prize for the 3-litre class.

September saw Duff, Clement and the bubbly Bertie Kensington Moir line up for sixteen laps of the Boulogne Circuit, run on 23 miles of rural roads. Boulogne is an historically important site for motor racing that is largely forgotten today; however, in its time it was one of the most rigorous tests of man and machine. Bentley did not fare well. Clement was out of the race by lap two with a burnt-out piston. Duff, driving the car in which he had competed at Le Mans, suffered the indignity, during the practice laps, of crashing into a cow — accounts of motor racing in those days are punctuated by stories of near misses and collisions involving slow-moving agricultural vehicles and livestock, which shared the same roads — as a result of which the car burst into flames while being driven in the race. Kensington Moir struggled with carburettor trouble, but at least completed the race, albeit well down the field.

It was the near-victory at Le Mans that had been the outstanding sporting achievement for the marque that year. Although not a win, it had attracted a good deal of attention to this young, but exciting British sports-car maker, bringing it to the notice of an eminent bacteriologist by the name of Dudley Benjafield. 'Benjy', as he quickly became known, was about the same age as W.O., but looked older, having been bald from a young age. Educated at Marlborough, then at University College Hospital and London University, he became a doctor in 1912 and by the 1920s was a respected consultant at St George's Hospital, London with a successful practice in Wimpole Street. He also enjoyed a reputation as a *bon vivant* and sportsman: married to a rich wife, whose family ran such useful things as the Savoy Hotel, Claridge's and the Cadogan, he was in the happy position of being able to indulge in the pastimes of the carefree amateur sportsman of the 1920s.

He was also an early follower of motor racing. 'I had always been very interested', he would later recall, 'and paid many visits to Brooklands in the early 1920s to watch with awe and admiration', little thinking that he himself might one day be 'hurtling round the rim of the track'.[9]

At that time, a participating role in motor racing simply did not occur to him. If anything, it seemed more likely that he would become involved with boating. During the early 1920s his chief pastime was *Lumière*, a 30-foot motorboat, which he kept moored at Folkestone on the Kent coast, where his relations ran a hotel. He and his wife would drive down to Folkestone most weekends, and in October 1923, aware of the sporting prowess of the Bentley, he bought himself a 3-litre, long chassis model

CHAPTER NINE

fitted with a body by Harrison's, in which he and his wife could make the journey. Over the course of that autumn he was seduced by the Bentley and its performance.

'She looked grand and behaved on the road like the thoroughbred she was. After two or three months' experience in handling her, I had no small opinion of my driving ability.'[100] Modest enough to ascribe his innate ability to the fact that the car 'came to hand so beautifully, with so little effort'[101], he soon found that, far more than just a method of getting from his laboratory to his motorboat, 'driving this car was great fun.'[102] He even began effecting racing gear-changes, learning 'the trick of dropping to third at speed with a quick double clutch and foot hard down all the time … I began to rather fancy myself.'[103] He even entered a hill climb. However, the decisive point in Benjy's progress towards motor racing came with the winter gales, when *Lumière* was 'battered to bits between two fishing smacks during an Easterly gale'.[104]

He was still looking for a replacement boat in the early spring of 1924 when he took his car to the Bentley service department at Cricklewood, where he met Kensington Moir, who was running the service side of the business in his own inimitable, fun-loving fashion. Bald Benjy and 'big, fat' Bertie obviously hit it off pretty instantly.[105] As well as the bond of the Bentley, the men shared a sunny and benevolent disposition and there was also mutual respect: the doctor was inclined 'to stand in fear and trepidation' of the skilful racing driver, who in turn appreciated the doctor's reputation as a medical man.[106]

One of the characteristics of the service department under Kensington Moir's despotic benevolence was the preferential treatment afforded to those whom he liked. Bertie at once put two mechanics on the car and said that the job could be done there and then.

'While waiting, I proceeded to pull his leg about the Bentley, suggesting that if I really wanted to go fast, that I should have to go elsewhere', recalled Benjy. Kensington Moir's normally cheery, rubicund features darkened. He did not think this at all funny. "Oh so you like going fast, do you?", asked Moir, sharply. By the tone of his voice, Benjy knew instantly that he had, to use his own evocative expression 'fired a mine' and he took the joke further, explaining that while he very much enjoyed travelling at speed, he would not think of selecting a Bentley for a fast run.

Moir grunted, grabbed Benjafield's arm and steered him towards a far corner of the workshop, where four mechanics were working on 'a dirty, dark-red car'. A serious racing machine, it was in fact the same nine-foot chassis car that Frank Clement had campaigned the previous season. "And so", said Moir menacingly, "You like going fast?" Benjafield felt he had gone too far, but there was no turning back and he replied, a little more

> As well as the bond of the Bentley, the men shared a sunny and benevolent disposition.

Dr. Benjafield and the Bentley. Benjafield in No. 7 (previous page), the car that went on to win the 1927 Le Mans, outside the Grand Hotel, Folkestone.

J.D. Benjafield, bacteriologist, in his Wimpole Street laboratory (opposite and overleaf) in the mid 1920s.

> 'Hardly had I gained my seat than he let in the clutch with a shriek, the back of the squab slammed into my spine and my head was nearly left behind on the track.'

fearfully this time, "Yes, I do." "Well, you see this car – I'm taking it down to Brooklands tomorrow afternoon, on test", said Moir, adding almost as an afterthought, "I'll take you round if you like."[107]

Neither man could back down. So the following day Benjy got through his work by lunchtime and, with no little trepidation, made his way out to Brooklands. Moir arrived at 2p.m. sharp with a mechanic, who at once set about 'changing over to track plugs and tightening up the shock-absorbers'.[108] As soon as these changes were made, Benjy was handed a pair of goggles and told to get into the car.

'Hardly had I gained my seat than he let in the clutch with a shriek, the back of the squab slammed into my spine and my head was nearly left behind on the track.'[109] The car was not even out of first gear and Benjy was regretting his little joke.

> The next five or six minutes were quite frightful; all Hell seemed to be let loose, engine and transmission screaming, and the car, as it seemed to my feverish imagination, bucketing all over the track. My goggles flew off and nearly strangled me and all I could do was pray that he might soon tire of this devil's play. After three or four laps, my supplications were heard and back we came to the paddock. Trembling like an aspen and feeling rather sick, I staggered out of the beastly thing; never had I been so utterly terrified.[110]

While Benjy quivered with fear and relief, Bertie roared with his customary good-humour.

> With his usually pleasant laugh, which now, however, sounded like a harsh cackle, he said, "Well, how do you like that, Doc?" Tremulously I whispered, "It was just fine." I feared he might still be able to hear my knees knocking together with fright, but, if he did, he omitted to say so, but, being the clever salesman that I have subsequently discovered him to be, I think that he was purposefully deaf, for his next remark was, "Well, how would you like to buy her?" I enquired the price and he quoted me some astronomical figure. He must have had me completely hypnotised for, without any demur, I agreed to take her. Thus was my introduction to motor-racing effected.[111]

Bentley badly needed amateurs like Benjafield, a man who could buy a racing car on a whim, having just been scared half to death after a brief test drive during which he had not even touched the wheel. Besides, Moir thought he had spotted potential beneath the doctor's bald dome and was determined to find out if Benjy had what it took to be a Bentley boy.

Although Moir thought he had discerned the makings of a racing driver, Benjy was not so sure. 'That evening, having recovered my normal sanity, I was filled with misgiving at what I had done. Here was I, a presumably respectable doctor, with amongst other things a

CHAPTER NINE

job on the staff of a teaching Medical School, committed to the control of a mechanical monster. Even the idea of being a passenger again terrified me.'[112]

All thoughts of a new motorboat gone, Benjy then spent two or three afternoons a week taking his new Bentley around Brooklands at ever increasing speeds, with a Bentley mechanic on hand to tune the engine. After three or four weeks, Moir suggested that the doctor enter his first race, at a small club meeting, with the mechanic riding with him to keep an eye on the controls and fuel pressure. Benjy did not know it, but this was in effect his try-out for the Bentley team.

> My instructions were not to exceed 3,400 revs., which was equal to a speed of about 96 m.p.h. This I proceeded to do and we completed the course without any incident, finishing fourth in the race. Both Browning and Moir seemed entirely satisfied and congratulated me; exactly why, I failed to understand, since fourth out of nine or ten starters did not, to me, appear to be any great achievement.[113]

Only later did he realise that to pass the test, he did not need to win this race, but simply to obey the instructions he had been given … which he had done in an exemplary fashion.

The next race was at the British Automobile Racing Club (B.A.R.C.) Whitsun meeting, by which time Benjy was feeling quite at home with his racing car. But while he was practising, his engine exploded and he had to retire to the pits with oil pouring out of the sump. It was four o'clock on Saturday afternoon; the race was less than 48 hours away. The remains of his dirty red car were towed back to the service department.

> 'Moir decided it was just possible to rebuild the engine in time for the race. With that, we all got down to the job with a will', recalled Benjy, who set himself the important task of going home to collect essential supplies in the shape of 'some bottles of champagne and masses of sandwiches'.[114]

Thus fortified, they continued work on the car until daybreak on Monday. Moir instructed Benjy to drive the car for 150 miles to run in the rebuilt engine and be at Brooklands at noon. Benjy drove to Folkestone for a hearty breakfast, then motored back to Brooklands, took his place on the starting line … and won. However, the hard weekend had taken its toll and by the end of the day Benjy was resting not on his victor's laurels, but in his bed, with a temperature of 103°.[115]

Benjy's winning streak continued into 1925, and on one spring morning, little more than a year after his first terrifying circuit of Brooklands with Moir, the phone rang. It was Moir, asking whether Benjy would be interested in driving for the firm at Le Mans.

Benjy had become a Bentley Boy.

> Little more than a year after his first terrifying circuit of Brooklands with Moir, the phone rang.

Chapter Ten

Before following Benjy's

progress to Le Mans,

it is important to fill in the gaps as to what had been happening at Bentley. At the time Benjy was buying his 3-litre racing car, W.O. was already working on a new generation of six-cylinder Bentleys.

To keep the spectators happy, circus performers and a boxing match were among the off-track diversions.

CHAPTER TEN

Sales of the 3-litre were good, causing Michael Hay to comment that 'from a commercial viewpoint, 1924 was in one important aspect at least, the most successful in Bentley Motors' history. More cars were manufactured (and sold) than in any other year.'[116] However, this apparently favourable statistic belied the true state of the company. Development costs of the new model were high and, in the words of one employee, 'all through 1924 the financial position was chaotic'.[117] Often Hillstead would find himself making the rounds of London agents offering advanced delivery dates or hefty discounts in the hope of getting a cheque to meet the weekly wage bill. When this did not work, H.M. Bentley – and even, on at least two occasions, Hillstead himself – would write personal cheques for £100 to keep things ticking over until the beginning of the following week. As Hillstead put it, 1924 was a year 'when the company could not buy a packet of cigarettes without increasing its overdraft'.[118]

The six-cylinder, 6½-litre car was a fabulous vehicle; 'the first in its class', according to Hillstead, 'to have a Jekyll and Hyde personality', and in this it was the true ancestor of the late twentieth- and early twenty-first-century Bentley super saloons with their luxurious four-door bodies and slingshot sports-car performance.[119] However, while W.O. was laying the foundations for a future he could never have imagined, it is questionable whether it was right for the immediate financial health of the company to invest so much money so early in the firm's life in an attempt to break into the luxury-car market, which had been dominated by the 40/50 Rolls-Royce – the Silver Ghost – which had first appeared on the market in 1906.

Moreover, while developing the 6½-litre car, W.O. was still committed to pursuing a racing programme, and come the 1924 Le Mans, Bentley was once again the only non-French marque to line up at the start.

Both Bentley and the race's organisers had learned from the inaugural race the preceding year. The date had been pushed back to the middle of June in the hope of avoiding the torrential rain that had dogged the race in 1923. To keep the spectators happy, circus performers and a boxing match were among the off-track diversions. There was also one significant change to the rules: open cars had to stop at the pits at the end of their fifth lap to raise their hood, after which they had to cover at least twenty laps with the hood deployed before returning to the pits to have the hood checked by race officials.

Thus, Duff – asked to drive again – added another dimension to his training: he practised raising and fixing his hood until he was so proficient as to be able to manage the whole manoeuvre in less than 40 seconds without needing to get out of the vehicle. Le Mans regulations decreed that only the driver was allowed to work on his car, and that included filling it up with petrol, oil and water – delivered not by pipe, but poured from cans heaved into position by the driver.

In addition to working on his physical fitness, Duff had lagged the petrol tank to protect against flying stones, and fitted a mesh grille to protect the

Duff's 3 Litre is worked on in the Bentley pits before the 1924 Le Mans race.

Duff refuelling his car during the 1924 Le Mans; Clement and Duff's car were to take first position.

headlamps and the honeycomb-shaped cooling elements of the radiator from the same hazard. It was out of this that the famous criss-cross pattern of the Bentley radiator grille developed.

W.O., too, took a more premeditated role in the affair, with the result that, despite an overlong pit stop caused by a swollen hubcap, Bentley won Le Mans. The response of the English spectators and press was rapturous; W.O.'s less so.

'The aftermath of that race was disappointing', complained Hillstead, with good reason:

> Having shaved and bathed, I looked forward to an evening of celebration. Duff and Clement had every right to be proud of their win; I had sent an enthusiastic wire to H.M. announcing the good news and, to my way of thinking, something in the nature of a feast was called for. Alas, it was a vain call. We dined in a private room; no one laughed; no one made any speeches; Moir ordered a bottle of champagne off his own bat; W.O. looked black, and the atmosphere of the gathering suggested humiliating defeat rather than victory.[120]

As soon as this morbid dinner was finished, they drove back to Dieppe. It seems that W.O. was far less well equipped to cope with victory than with adversity, of which he faced plenty on his return to London.

The financial status of the company became increasingly parlous as the year wore on and there were only so many times that Hillstead could make his desperate dashes round the London agents with the promise of a discounted chassis delivered early in exchange for immediate payment.

The constant precariousness was wearing for all, but particularly for W.O. In his 1958 autobiography, he offers a rare insight into his emotional state:

CHAPTER TEN

The trouble was that Bentley Motors was everything to me. All my ambitions were contained in that car, and the designing, building and perfecting of it were my whole life, occupying all my waking thoughts and every minute of my days. In those critical formative years of the company, when the loss of my wife still lay heavily on me and there was no gentle cushion of domesticity to support me and absorb the shock of the reaction after a hard day's work, I am sure I was not easy company. I was taciturn, unresponsive and over-sensitive to criticism, and in the intimacy of the board room these characteristics became more marked and I was at my worst.

Normally if I was cross, dissatisfied with something, or if I disagreed with someone, I might either mutter inaudibly or express myself in total silence, all of which was perfectly understood by the men at the works; I hated rows and violent words, which were nervously exhausting and took your mind off your work. Unfortunately I couldn't do this in board meetings; I was supposed to talk and explain and justify, feeling all the time I was being forced to make excuses for myself and others when I felt that none was required, begging for things which should have been offered, always on the defensive, a situation I detest.[121]

W.O.'s identity was so bound up in the work he did at Bentley that he was intolerant of those who did not share his remarkable dedication; and with this came a sense of entitlement that did not fit at all with the financial circumstances. In the workshops he was a hero. Time and again in memoirs from the factory floor of that era, the image portrayed of W.O. is that of a distant, softly spoken character, 'the Great Man' as many called him, an omnipotent, omniscient hero to the men who worked for him. However, as the only engineer on the board, he felt cornered and misunderstood when dealing with his fellow directors. W.O. was building a dream. What others saw was a small under-financed carmaker with serious problems.

By 1925 it was clear that a new owner would need to be sought for Bentley Motors if the company was to continue trading. And the resourceful Hillstead had an idea of a man who might well be interested in acquiring a motor manufacturer with a racing team. The man he had in mind was not yet 30 years old but was already in possession of a considerable fortune, and had just benefited from a will being settled in his favour to the tune of nearly one million pounds. Moreover, the young man in question was acquiring a reputation as a useful amateur motor-racing driver. A Brooklands habitué from its reopening after the war, he was also a Bentley customer.

W.O. made the initial contact and then Hillstead was deputed to drive down to the young man's country house, a sprawling newly built stately home called Ardenrun near Lingfield in Surrey, on the pretext of showing him the new 6½-litre Bentley.

The name of this rich young man who was destined to become the owner of Bentley Motors was Woolf Barnato.

> By 1925 it was clear that a new owner would need to be sought for Bentley Motors if the company was to continue trading.

Chapter Eleven

This trowel
was used by
Miss Gerda von Chappuis
&
Mrs Fritz Achelis
when laying
the
Foundations stone
of
The House
on
Ardenrun Place.
August 1st 1906.
❖❖❖

So runs the inscript
due Edwardian flou

on a silver-bladed, ivory-handled trowel in the private collection of John
Lingfield, Surrey, that served as a de facto country club for the Bentley

ion, engraved with
rish and furbelow,

Konig. Ardenrun was the spectacular Carolean-style mansion near
Boys during Woolf Barnato's time at the helm of the company.

AN UNCERTAIN FUTURE

CHAPTER ELEVEN

In his day Konig was a keen competitive driver, racing a Bentley special – a 1926 3-litre chassis fitted with an 8-litre Bentley engine – with some success. However, it is not the Bentley connection that ties him to this Edwardian trowel, but a family link. Gerda von Chappuis was his grandmother, who subsequently married Frederick Adolphus Konig. Together with his elder brother, Hans Henry, Frederick ran a successful bank in the City, which added to an already considerable fortune.

Ardenrun was Hans Henry's country place, although he was rarely there; his frail constitution and immense fortune militated against spending too much time in England so he retired to a villa on the French Riviera in Menton. His brother already had one stately home, Tyringham Hall in Buckinghamshire, designed by John Soane, and had no need of another. The newly built and splendidly appointed Ardenrun was surplus to family requirements.

The advertisement, placed by 'Messrs. Trollop, Estate and Land Agents' in *Country Life* on 15 November 1919, giving notice of the proposed auction of the house, offers some idea of the scale of Ardenrun.

The post-war millionaire in search of a country seat, with the ready-made lifestyle of a country gentleman to slip into, was invited to place his bid for this 'exquisite modern mansion', described as 'the very choice freehold residential estate known as Ardenrun Place'. 'Approached by a long drive with lodge', Ardenrun was 'replete with every possible convenience'. The future squire would not be troubled with the many vexations of an ancient country house or crumbling stately home in need of restoration. As well as the 'ample and well arranged accommodation' there

> The post-war millionaire in search of a country seat, with the ready-made lifestyle of a country gentleman to slip into, was invited to place his bid.

Woolf Barnato's country residence Ardenrun (below, left and previous page), a mini-stately home built by the Konig family.

was 'electric light, company's water, central heating' and – the *dernier cri* of early twentieth-century technology – 'telephone'.

As well as the impressive façade and various wings of the house, accompanying photographs illustrate cavernous, imposing rooms: dining room, music room, lounge hall, tapestry hall – in each the furnishings are dwarfed by the scale of the place. Beyond the walls of the house were 'delightful pleasure grounds', a kitchen garden, 'first-class stabling and garages', an unspecified number of cottages and a home farm ('with bailiff's house and excellent buildings'), all set on 347 acres.

Constructed during the last great phase of British country-house building, Ardenrun was designed by Ernest Newton, a protégé of the great Victorian master Norman Shaw, to mirror the tastes of the landed gentry at a time when Great Britain was the unchallenged world superpower with an empire that reached over one third of the globe. Ardenrun was a world away from the slums of Whitechapel in the East End of London; yet that was exactly where Woolf Barnato's father, Barney, had been born in 1852.

Victorian England is often seen as a society codified by a rigid class system that provided a place for everyone and kept everyone in his or her place. As the story of Barney Barnato shows, this was only part of the truth. There were opportunities for social mobility: a man could be born a pauper, yet through industry, ambition, skulduggery or luck could end his days a millionaire and a baronet, if not quite a gentleman – that took a generation or two.

Even by the standards of the age, Barney Barnato's rise was remarkable. Son of a second-hand clothes trader called Isaac Isaacs, Barnett Isaacs wanted more from life than the opportunity to speculate in worn frock coats and shabby top hats.[122] Stage-struck as a youth, he used to beg the theatre tickets of those leaving the performance early, to sell them on to those who arrived late. Strong and dextrous, he trained as a juggler and a boxer, changed his name to Barney Barnato and even tried his hand at acting.

His elder brother went out to South Africa shortly after diamonds had been discovered there, and in the early 1870s Barney followed him, equipped, depending on which report you read, with £25 or £50, and 40 boxes of cigars.

Shrewd, charming, physically resilient and almost totally without social polish, Barnato flourished in the booming years of South African diamond mines and gold fields. In 1874 he founded the firm of Barnato Brothers, which opened a London office in 1880; 1888 saw the formation of De Beers Consolidated Mines, with Barnato and Cecil Rhodes as life governors. The late 1880s found him buying gold mines on a massive scale and when he returned to London in 1895, the Lord Mayor of London threw a banquet in his honour a mile or so from where his father had sold second-hand clothes.

Yet all his life, Barney felt something of an outsider. 'Rhodes looks down on me because I have no education – never been to College like him', he once said of his contemporary. 'If I had received the education of

Cecil Rhodes there would not have been a Cecil Rhodes.¹²³' At least one historian felt this statement was 'by no means a vain boast'.¹²⁴

However, he never aped the manners of those who looked down on him and he spent his money with a carefree and cheerful vulgarity that must have appalled those who considered themselves his betters. He had lived with Fanny Bees for many years, but only when she became pregnant with their first child in 1892 did the couple marry and move to London. He bought himself a site on Park Lane, and drew up plans for an extravagant five-storey mansion with a ballroom, a brace of billiard rooms, a statement staircase of marble and so on. When it was finished it stood out like a beacon. 'Everybody who passes down Park Lane', it was said, 'was reminded, by a certain house sprawling with naked nymphs and cupids, that the shortest way from Whitechapel to Mayfair crossed and re-crossed the Equator.'¹²⁵ While he was waiting for this palace to be completed, he made his family as comfortable as possible in Spencer House in St James's, the London palace of the Earls Spencer, which he rented as temporary accommodation and in which Woolf, his third child, was born in September 1895.

Barnato may never have been accepted into Society, but it was impossible for him to remain unnoticed and he was even immortalised in a music-hall ditty, the refrain of which included the lines

> I tell you straight, he's up to date,
> Is beautiful, bountiful Barney!¹²⁶

Rich, powerful and if not famous, then at least notorious, Barney Barnato was a remarkable man, who might well have eclipsed Rhodes had he lived long enough, but by the summer of 1897 he was dead. The end was sudden. In 1886, after the failure of a bank he had founded, he became depressed and started drinking heavily, was unable to sleep, lost interest in his appearance and even the construction of his Park Lane palace. He turned up at Southampton to see a relative off wearing dress trousers, a sports coat and a fur overcoat, and on the spur of the moment boarded the same boat and sailed for South Africa, where his state of mind deteriorated further. Joined there by his wife and children, he started imagining that attempts were being made on their lives, and in one delirious spell started to claw at the walls looking for hidden diamonds. Doctors advised a break from work and the family set sail for England. At first he behaved normally on board, then became increasingly worried and could not be left alone. On 14 June it seems that he suffered an acute attack of paranoia and, with a cry "They're after me", he leapt overboard.¹²⁷ The coroner's verdict was of 'Death by drowning while temporarily insane'.¹²⁸ The ship's fourth officer leapt in after him and tried to save him, and a lifeboat was launched, but Barnato was found floating face down and could not be revived.

His funeral was as epic as his life: 200 carriages followed his coffin when he was buried in Willesden on 19 June 1897. He was not quite 45 years

Ardenrun's games room and conservatory, Barnato's famed party venue that was destroyed by fire.

Barnato prior to racing at Le Mans, with Clement (far left) and Birkin (seated, centre).

old. Almost as soon as he was dead, rumours started circulating that he had been murdered. Paranoid or not, he had certainly made enemies and his business transactions were often controversial, to say the least. Moreover, someone had testified to hearing a cry of murder at the time he went overboard, and the fatal shooting of one of his nephews nine months later revived the theories of foul play, which still enjoy some currency today.

As a common-law-wife and then legal spouse, Fanny Barnato had kept out of the public eye, something she continued to do as a widow, devoting herself to the upbringing of her three children, who enjoyed a pleasant but surprisingly unspoilt life, considering the manner in which their father had lived and died. The widow and her children divided their time between a house in Colwyn Bay in north Wales, a London flat near Marble Arch and a seaside villa on the south coast at Brighton, where Woolf and his brother Jack spent their holidays from Charterhouse. Their sister Leah seems to have inherited her father's love of the performing arts and married first a violinist then a silent-film star before descending into alcoholism. Jack was a pilot in the First World War, bombed Constantinople, was mentioned in despatches and died of pneumonia in October 1918.

Woolf, powerfully built and given the sobriquet 'Babe' (either a reference to his position as the third and last of the children, or an ironic glance at his stocky six-foot frame), made a name for himself at Cambridge, 'flooring the heaviest of boxing Blues'. It was soon agreed that he was 'one of the greatest all-round athletes of his generation'.[129] During the war he enlisted as a private and eventually became a captain, serving in Palestine. Once hostilities were over, he cultivated his passion for fast cars and fashionable women.

CHAPTER ELEVEN

It was through the intervention of his old commanding officer, who lived in a house on the Ardenrun estate, that Woolf secured the house. According to Rivers Fletcher, by the time Hillstead was sent to show Barnato the new 6½-litre, the original estate advertised in *Country Life* had been expanded to around 1,000 acres, which included a golf course. By now married to and divorced from the daughter of an eminent Wall Street financier, Woolf Barnato was already well on his way to becoming the leading playboy of his generation. As befitted a man of that station, he was still asleep when Hillstead made his way up the long drive at Ardenrun.

Roused from bed, Barnato took the car for a test drive then settled to business over lunch. He was plainly interested in buying the company, but not at any old price: in addition to having inherited a congenital family shrewdness, Barnato was well advised. He had a great deal of money and, although he may have thrown some of it about seducing actresses and giving parties, the majority was closely shepherded. He was more a sportsman than a businessman, but he was most certainly not a rich young fool ready to be parted from his money. In fact, Barnato's personal relationship with money was quite the opposite: according to some accounts, he was notoriously rather mean, in public at least.

He may have entertained lavishly and lived well, but Barnato disliked lending money and, according to W.O., who got to know him as well as any man, his behaviour was characterised by an 'extraordinary parsimony over little things, which made it impossible, for example, for him ever to offer anyone a cigarette'[130] from the gold case that he carried in a specially tailored pocket of his suits.[131] Apparently Bertie Kensington Moir did once manage to get a cigarette out of Barnato, but claimed 'to carry the scars from the flange of that gold case across his knuckles' for life.[132]

Hillstead came away from Ardenrun with the impression that a deal could easily be done, although he had mixed feelings about the young man's prospective purchase of the marque into which he had invested a little capital and a considerable amount of effort and enthusiasm.

> Was I pleased? Yes, and no. Barnato could put Bentley Motors on its feet without feeling the strain; on the other hand, he could take it up as a toy, have his fun, and then throw it to one side when the novelty had worn off. As I saw the picture, the whole issue depended upon the company's ability to get on its feet during the novelty period, and to what extent W.O. was prepared to play ball with Barnato's financial advisers. Two chartered accountants – one a Scot, the other a Jew – who had no other interests than to do the best for the man who employed them, could well be both formidable and exacting. I decided to wait and see, and my waiting and seeing were largely influenced by the happenings at Le Mans during that same year of 1925.[133]

> He was more a sportsman than a businessman, but he was most certainly not a rich young fool ready to be parted from his money.

CHAPTER TWELVE

Le Mans 1925 was

different: it began with the Le Mans start,

for which drivers sprinted across the track to their cars and started them up – a practice that ended only in 1969. Moreover, Bentley's victory the preceding year had raised the profile of the race internationally and there were 68 entries, including two from the USA, six from Britain and seven from Italy. In the event, 49 cars were to start the race, and among them was the first works entry from Bentley, which Benjafield had been asked to drive by Bertie Kensington Moir, who would be his co-driver. Duff was back again, paired with Clement, who was driving, as usual, his own car.

Between 1925 and 1969, all the Le Mans races began with a sprint start. The 1930 race (above) was no exception.

AN UNCERTAIN FUTURE

This time there were plenty of other noted British drivers, including leading jockey and racing driver George Duller and the irrepressible Sammy Davis. Irrespective of team loyalties, these men were friends and it was natural that they would get together and socialise.

The atmosphere before that Le Mans was light-hearted, with plenty of practical jokes involving competitors' cars. And even Benjy's attempt at physical fitness ended comically when he attempted to walk round the course and collapsed at the White House turn; he 'returned at last on a lorry, never again to preach the advantages of exercise!'[134]

Having seen what the fierce heat had done to Benjy, Duller, Sammy, Moir, Benjy and W.O. took a taxi ride around the track to compare notes. 'At least, that was the idea', recalled Sammy Davis:

> Unfortunately someone told the cab driver that we were "coureurs" of the great race, with the awful result that he decided to show what he could do. After the first corner conversation became incoherent, after the second I decided it was best to keep one's eyes shut, at the third George leant out of the window and cried desperately "Allez, slower!" Only the first word bit home [sic], resulting in an awful skid at Arnage S turn, during which the body of the cab began to come off. Unanimously the representatives of two famous teams decided to stop at the first café, there to present the driver, and themselves, with several drinks, pay what was needed, and walk home.[135]

However, the light-hearted mood did not last long into the race. For the Bentley team, confidence must have been considerable. Preparations were perhaps too careful: fuel was calculated minutely to give cars the best advantage, but W.O. had not factored in the effect of the raised hood, or the presence of Henry Segrave – arguably the greatest driver of his generation – at the wheel of a Sunbeam. Refuelling was forbidden during the first twenty laps, but right after the beginning of the race, Moir got involved in a duel with Segrave and ran out of petrol before the twentieth lap, putting him out of the race before Benjy had even had a chance to drive.

The same happened to John Duff, who dashed back to the pits for more fuel. When W.O. pointed out that this was against the rules, Duff replied most vigorously that "it's my car and I'll do what I damn well like with it".[136] He got it started again, but by the early morning it had caught fire and, although he had smothered the flames with his cushion while driving, it was judged that repairs would take too long. The second Bentley was out of the race.

It was a disaster. If W.O. was morose while presiding over the previous year's victory dinner, his mood at what he himself called '"black" Le Mans' can only be guessed.[137]

It was Duff's last Le Mans, but not his last track outing in a Bentley. In September 1925 he smashed the world speed record over 24 hours, driving his Bentley at the oval track of Montlhéry near Paris, the French riposte to Brooklands. A total of 2,280.69 miles were covered, which, as *The Motor* of 29 September pointed out, was 'a distance almost equivalent to six times the journey from London to Edinburgh'. It was an impressive achievement and significant for the future of Bentley Motors in that Duff's co-driver was Captain Woolf Barnato.

In the end, Barnato made his offer for the company in May of 1926. His terms 'included the devaluation of the existing £1 shares to a shilling, which meant a nasty knock for many of us', recorded W.O. blithely.[138]

For W.O., the loss of money was of little importance. Keeping Bentley running was his only concern, and with Barnato at the wheel, he imagined that all financial concerns were at an end and he would no longer have to suffer the indignity of going begging to a board of unsympathetic directors. Others were less pleased; H.M. Bentley and Hillstead were among those who resigned.

> Moir got involved in a duel with Segrave and ran out of petrol.

It is with some callousness, perhaps unintentional, that W.O. recorded this in his autobiography, saying that 'The broom was forcefully wielded' and Hillstead and H.M. 'decided that the new regime was unlikely to suit them'.[139] H.M. was after all his brother and had played his protective role superbly, helping his younger sibling realise his dream and doing his best to shield him from the realities of running a car company during an increasingly uncertain economic period. But for W.O., family and friends came a poor second to cars, and at that time he seemed to care much more for machines than he did for people.

In his defence, it must be said that there was little he could do. Had Barnato not bought the company, it would probably have gone into liquidation, so Bentley had no room to negotiate terms. The economic situation of Great Britain was dire – just how bad became evident very quickly. As Barnato took over the company, the country was thrown into chaos by the General Strike. Unrest among the workers had reached a critical level and, given the events in Russia only nine years earlier, there must have been many who feared that a Communist revolution and a civil war were on the way.

As things turned out, it was a very British affair. Although there was certainly upheaval, the strike did not bring about national collapse, nor even manage to stop the Chelsea Flower Show, which was merely postponed for a week. The fear of a nation paralysed by a strike-hit rail network never materialised, in part due to the 'mucking in' of rich motorists, among them Woolf Barnato.

One of the many aspects of British life that was thrown into sharp relief by this nationwide industrial action was its reliance on the railways. In the middle of the nineteenth century, Britain had experienced a railway boom, and by the early twentieth century, when W.O. was working on the railways, trains connected almost every part of Britain, however remote or apparently inconsequential. The motorcar was still at that time considered a hazardous eccentricity.

However, by the mid-1920s things had changed. The rail network still moved agricultural produce and consumer goods to the cities, raw materials and fuel to factories, newspapers and mail to the furthest parts of the country and so on. But the road network was

Kimberley mines cheque; Barnato's lucrative diamond dealings funded his takeover of Bentley Motors.

increasingly well developed, so that during the General Strike, much of the work of the rail system was transferred to the roads. It is probably during the General Strike that the balance of transport began to shift from rail to road. As the 'White Line' correspondent of the *Sporting Life* put it, 'Among the potent factors which went most entirely to break the strike, and which completely upset the plans of the strikers' leaders, none played a greater part than road transport.' He went on to add that in the future a 'railway strike, while it may occasion the fear of some inconvenience, will never again be regarded as a serious menace to industry or to the travelling public'.[140]

Indeed for many Society and motor-sport figures, the General Strike was a bit of a lark. Malcolm Campbell found himself driving a train; John Cobb, who went on to hold the land-speed record, drove a bus, as did racing driver Kaye Don; there was even talk that some of the more high-spirited emergency bus drivers enjoyed racing each other, irrespective of schedules, stops and passengers who wanted to dismount. Typical was the experience of one member of the Bentley company, who found himself driving a bus in the Knightsbridge area:

> It was lunch time and as he happened to live in Eaton Square and, so far as he could see, there were no passengers aboard, he was tempted to leave the advertised route and partake of a little

food under his own roof. Needless to say the conductor – also suffering the pangs of hunger – readily agreed to a temporary retirement from duty. But at the very moment when the conspirators were entering the house, they spotted one lone passenger sitting on the top and obviously puzzled at the unfamiliar surroundings.

"As you're here you'd better come and have lunch with us," said the owner of the house. And that was precisely what the passenger did.[141]

Naturally Barnato was doing something much more glamorous than driving a bus. Within 48 hours of the strike he had helped the police to form the 'Brooklands Squad', a team of crack racing drivers, with cars 'capable of speeds from 90 to 100 miles an hour'[142] attached to Scotland Yard and entrusted with delivering sensitive government documents at high speed. Among the volunteers were Mr Frazer Nash, well-known jockey George Duller, Le Mans driver Henry Segrave and others.

'All the "Brooklands Squad" rendered valuable service to the police and some remarkable feats were performed', wrote the *Daily Mail*. 'Capt. Woolf Barnato took an urgent message from London to Birmingham, a distance of approx- imately 106 miles, in 2 hrs 11 mins., his running time being only 11 mins in excess of the average express train.'[143]

After the strike broke, a demobilisation lunch was held and the men paraded their cars at New Scotland Yard. It was just the sort of stuff Babe loved, and the photograph of the Brooklands Squad shows a smiling Barnato clad in a leather trench coat. Their duty to the nation done, Barnato and George Duller drove into town to go night-clubbing.

Small, lithe, tough and muscular, with a springiness to his movements and rugged weather-beaten features, George Duller was typical of the men Babe Barnato counted as his friends and who would soon become known in the popular imagination as the high-living Bentley Boys. Described as the 'life and soul'[144] with an impish, irreverent sense of humour, a cheery grin and an endless repertoire of stories from the world of racing, he could be counted on to raise spirits wherever he was. But his wicked sense of humour did not eclipse his prowess as a jump jockey and a racing driver. He won his first horse race aged seven and acquired a reputation as an excellent jockey who also turned his hand to other sports. It was said that while driving he would occasionally rise in his seat as if on horseback. For him, motor racing was a way of keeping fit and mentally alert between horse races, and in one year alone he owned 48 cars at one time or another. He was a keen aviator too. "Flying", said Duller, "comes naturally to anyone who can ride. It's all in the touch and is simply a case of hands, as in driving."[145]

Although nothing like as rich as Babe, Duller had something Barnato valued more than money – remarkable sporting ability. Mutual respect was the foundation for a friendship that saw Duller and his wife spending most weekends at Ardenrun, and Duller accompanying Barnato on his nocturnal roistering around town.

Pulling up that night in Cork Street, a street known for its high concentration of prostitutes, and also coincidentally the location of the new, expanded Bentley showroom, 'Pollen House', Duller's bag was stolen from the car. As the *Evening News* informed its readers the following morning, the bag had 'contained his evening clothes, his links and his studs'. However, neither Duller nor Barnato let the theft put them off a good night out. 'When later in the evening the pair turned up at the Ambassador Club Mr. Duller was in borrowed kit. He danced, but not with his usual smoothness, for the boots he wore were made for a man six inches taller than himself.'[146]

Close to Hanover Square and therefore also to the Bentley offices, the Ambassador Club was a new addition to London nightlife during the 1920s. It opened on 28 January 1926 'under the guiding intelligence of M. Rizzo, formerly of the Savoy and Cairo's', and the inaugural dinner was well attended, with guests including Lady Birkenhead, Signor Marconi, Gilbert Frankie, Louis Greg and Woolf Barnato.[147] Barnato liked the Ambassador, spending quite a bit of time there in the early part of 1926, so it was natural that, after the excitement of the General Strike, he and Duller would go there to unwind over a bottle or two of Champagne … after all, as well as being one of its most assiduous patrons, Barnato was, along with the Colonel Selby-Lowness, known to be one of the club's founders. Now he had a sports-car company to go with his nightclub business.

The Bentley showrooms (above), in 1927, at Pollen House on Cork Street with three 3 Litres and one 6 1/2 Litre.

The Brooklands Squad (below), Barnato's crack team of racing drivers who aided Scotland Yard during the General Strike.

OR SPEEDING FOR POLICE.—Members of the "Brooklands Squad" of racing motorists who made journeys at speed for Scotland Yard during the strike. Right to left, Commander Temperley, Mr. G. Duller, Lord Rossmore, Messrs. R. S. Dyball, H. O. D. Segrave, P. G. A. Harvey and W. Barnato. Extreme left, Mr. G. Callingham.

PART THREE

On the road to glory

CHAPTER THIRTEEN

As well as money, Barnato was to bring glamour to Bentley Motors.

True, the company may have, in W.O.'s words, 'ceased to be a tight, loyal, if occasionally bickering, family unit'.[148] Instead, it metamorphosed into a highly fashionable, if slightly raffish, organisation frequented by rich young men who sought the thrills of high-speed motoring.

The 1929 Le Mans Bentley team, photographed at Mount Street Public Gardens in the heart of Mayfair, a stone's throw from 'Bentley Corner' on Berkley Square.

The complexion of the company changed at once now the offices above the showroom on Cork Street were stuffed with Barnato's chums. One of them, the Marquis of Casa Maury, who had driven a Bugatti at the T.T. in Ireland four years earlier, was appointed joint managing director with W.O. 'Although he was an astute business man, he gave the impression of being a social butterfly, a gay, light-hearted aristocrat with plenty of money of his own, a taste for the arts, a man who "knew everyone"'.[149] Like the new owner of Bentley Motors, his reputation was that of a man's man, a ladies' man and a man-about-town, which was pretty much the job description of the Jazz Age rat-pack known as the Bentley Boys.

Barnato may have been to a major public school and Cambridge, but he was not, to use the term as Hillstead employed it, a 'public-school man'. He enjoyed life too much, lived it too well and was too much of a man-of-the-world to concern himself overly with the world of the old-school tie. And while W.O. was happy to spend Barnato's money investing in a renewed racing programme and the development of further models, he had his doubts about Barnato's standing as a gentleman. Barnato may have called Ardenrun his 'country residence', observed W.O. a trifle spiffily, 'but I thought it was more like the Savoy, swarming as it always was with maids and footmen and valets in every corridor'.[150]

Under Barnato, Ardenrun was not the traditional English country house its builder had envisaged. Instead it was turned into – quite literally – a playboy's mansion. Barnato built a full-size, mock-Tudor pub in the house's rambling basement, where small, leaded windows with diamond panes, behind which were electric lights, gave the impression of daylight, and a large oak-beamed fireplace was hung with pewter tankards. Depending on the time of day, or night, visitors would encounter either hunting folk fortifying themselves with hearty helpings of bacon and eggs, tipsy show-business types or carousing racing drivers.

There was even an improvised circuit for the houseguests. The course ran down the front drive to a pond by the estate's farmhouse, past stables and kennels, over a bridge and then down the half mile straight that was the back drive. Drivers would be expected to return on the same course, avoiding oncoming drivers by going a different direction around the pond – an instruction to which not every driver would adhere!

Barnato was as fond of wagers as he was of practical jokes. One evening, after an excellent dinner at Ardenrun (twenty or thirty sitting down to dinner was the norm), he contrived that Duller and Benjafield should bet that each could make a faster Le Mans start than the other. In order to resolve the dispute, it was suggested that the Le Mans start should be replicated on the drive and that the two men should stand on one side of the drive and, when the flag was dropped, should sprint across the drive, leap into their cars, start them and drive off. The first to accomplish the task would be the winner.

It is easy to imagine the amusement at the sight of the small, lithe jockey with his weather-beaten features, and the respected, bald, Harley Street specialist, each in evening clothes, poised as if ready to begin the 24-hour race at Le Mans, surrounded by a large crowd of dinner guests – actors, actresses, café-society types – all in various states of intoxication. The flag was dropped. 'Urged by hilarious applause both ran like the wind and jumped in successfully, no mean feat in the circumstances. But, alas, nothing could make the engine of George's car even try to start, while that of Benjy started with a roar but nothing would make the car move whatever gear was tried.'[151] With the other guests now helpless with mirth, the two racing drivers realised that they had been 'had'. 'Some person or persons unknown had separated the contact points of one [car] with an insulator, and jacked a rear wheel of the other clear of the ground.'[152]

Like a character from a novel by Waugh or Scott Fitzgerald, Barnato was the gatekeeper to a world of fun. At a time when a working man earned three or four pounds a week, if he could get work, Barnato would fritter his way through £800 a week in just living his life the way he liked it – fast. 'His image was that of a multi-millionaire playboy', according to one who went to work for him at Bentley Motors, 'whose girlfriends were stars of stage and screen rather than the eligible debs'.[153]

Following his divorce, Barnato thoroughly enjoyed life as a bachelor. Mothers of 'nice' girls were very

CHAPTER THIRTEEN

His reputation was that of a man's man, a ladies' man and a man-about-town, which was pretty much the job description of the Jazz Age rat-pack known as the Bentley Boys.

careful were he was concerned. 'My mother was very strict about where I went and with whom. For instance, she did not approve of my going to the famous weekend parties given by Woolf ('Babe') Barnato; I was only allowed to go there for the day', recalled one Society beauty many years later. 'Babe's reputation with women was rather suspect, and this was why my mother didn't approve of my staying at his house.'[154]

As he settled into life as chairman of Bentley Motors, Babe's harem included Bentleys as well as girls, the former overseen by his chauffeur Cyril du Heaume. At Ardenrun there were, of course, plenty of garages, but when Barnato came to London, two or three of his personal cars were stabled in the basement of the company's offices at Pollen House. In the morning, or whenever it was he awoke, he would call over for whichever of his cars he fancied using that day. As the distance from Cork Street to his flat in Grosvenor Square was just a few minutes' drive, this task was usually entrusted to a junior member of staff. One day the job fell to the young Rivers Fletcher.

> To reach Grosvenor Square from Cork Street, I usually drove down Bruton Street to Berkeley Square, hanging the tail out and feeling like Le Mans, when I lost it, completely. The Bentley swung right round and hit a taxi head on. Nobody was hurt but both cars were an awful mess. A policeman appeared from nowhere but apparently he had not seen me dicing. I apologized to the cabby and he was very decent, saying that he reckoned he would get a new taxi off my insurance. The chairman's 4½ [the car that effectively replaced the 3-litre[155]] looked a sorry sight, with the front axle pushed back and the radiator gushing water over the block. I felt dreadful: I had done it all in one – my job, my career and the chairman's 4½ .

Feeling understandably sick, Fletcher ran back to the offices, but when he told his boss what he had done, his boss was too frightened to call Barnato. Instead he instructed the youngster to take the firm's demonstration model round and explain what had happened.

> At Grosvenor Square the butler kept me waiting in the hall, every minute making me feel even worse. Eventually I was ushered upstairs to where Barnato was having his breakfast. Sitting beside him was a gorgeous blonde whom I recognized immediately. I did not know her, I was not in that league at all, but I had seen the show in which she was one of the stars.
>
> It is reassuring to note that while his employees were hard at work, the chairman was filling his time in a useful manner.
>
> I remember explaining how wet it was and how I thought someone must have spilled some oil on the road in Berkeley Square. Every time I looked up the Captain was scowling at me over the top of his egg. Then, when I reached the part of my story when I told him how I shunted his 4½ into that taxi, that beautiful blonde put her hand on the chairman's shoulder and smiled at him. Barnato turned and grinned back at her ... He turned to me, still with a grin on his face, and said, "Now, Rivers, you will never do that again. Run along."[156]

Apart from the enduring image of the international playboy enjoying breakfast with a gorgeous musical star, at a time when his employees were already hard at work, this vignette is eloquently expressive of Barnato's temperament. While he might have been parsimonious when it came to standing a round of drinks or offering a cigarette, he could be immensely magnanimous. He knew that he could not say anything that would make Rivers Fletcher feel any worse, but contented himself with a mild rebuke. Moreover, demonstrating that he still trusted the young man, a few weeks later when the car had been repaired, he asked Fletcher to deliver it to Ardenrun.

This story shows that Barnato's love of women and passion for cars were never far from each other. There was even one constructed expressly with women in mind.

> Amongst Barnato's Bentleys was a great big Standard Six with a unique limousine body by Thrupp and Maberly. This car was reserved for evening use and was driven exclusively by Cyril du Heaume. The front compartment was a single seater only, in the same way as applies to a London taxi, but the left side was not open for luggage but built into the rest of the body, making a large L-shaped boudoir. This 'room' had windows with blinds so that the boudoir could be totally enclosed.[157]

Typical of the women he entertained in the back of this sumptuously appointed vehicle was musical star June Howard-Tripp, whose hit songs included the entirely appropriate 'Ladies are Running Wild'. June and Woolf made a stunning couple. Photographs show that he was a very good-looking man, described as 'a laughing, mahogany-tanned cavalier with wavy dark hair' and brown eyes, who 'stood over six foot but looked shorter because of his stocky and muscular build'.[158] June was the opposite, with fine but animated features, smooth fair hair, blue eyes and a creamy complexion.

Barnato's life could be followed vicariously through the pages of Society magazines such as the *Tatler* and the *Sphere*. Many of his friends would today be described as 'celebrities', including Fred Astaire and Jack Buchanan, the latter the owner of a Speed Six and the first of the production 8-litre cars. While from the beginning Bentley had been a car aimed at the sporting gentleman and the young aristocrat (both the Prince of Wales and Prince George drove Bentleys), it was Barnato, with his impressive social circle and his links across the Atlantic, that made the car an international must-have.

In his autobiography, W.O. smugly related that the register of Bentley customers 'began to look like an anthology of *Debrett* and the *Directory of Directors*. Tallulah Bankhead, Gertrude Lawrence, Beatrice Lillie all had Bentleys, and it became almost a routine for visiting American film and stage stars – and many Eastern potentates and European royalty too – to go home with one.'[159] W.O. might have liked to think that the marque's reputation of sound engineering and racing success was responsible for such an illustrious client list: in reality it is more likely that Barnato's reputation as a playboy and socialite and his enthusiasm for being seen with young starlets had more to do with Bentley's fashionable status.

While such associations may have been looked down upon in some quarters, the more emancipated spirits of the era enjoyed the frisson of Bohemia that came from hanging out with actors, actresses, singers, film stars and, of course, heroes of the race-track.

At that time, racing drivers held a unique place in the public imagination and were even considered leaders of fashion by their admirers. Rivers Fletcher was very taken with the way one driver wore his hair, brushed back from the face unparted. 'I tried to copy this but my parents were horrified and would not allow me to wear my hair in such an outlandish style.'[160] On another occasion, Rivers was taken with a stylish accessory favoured by the racing fraternity:

> I very much admired the black and white check caps worn by Jack[161] and his younger brother Clive, another very tall and handsome fellow. On the very next day I bought one for myself. When my father saw me wearing it, he said, 'good heavens! You look like the paper boy. You're not nearly tall enough for an imitation of Jack Dunfee. Take it off at once!' He was right of course, dammit! I was prey to this absurd adulation for people in the world of motor racing that made me want to copy them.[162]

Not all drivers, however, were capable of inspiring young men to follicular folly and sartorial stupidity. And that was the most marked difference between W.O. and Barnato; at that time W.O. lived for his cars; Barnato, rather, lived for the enjoyment of life.

Barnato tinkering with a car, aided by a friend and watched on by his wife June.

CHAPTER THIRTEEN

CHAPTER FOURTEEN

Much as

he enjoyed himself, Barnato was no dissolute gallant.

A true Corinthian, he boxed, shot, rode, hunted, played golf, raced powerboats and drove. Sammy Davis appraised the new owner of Bentley Motors as follows:

> Woolf Barnato ... could in strength and tenacity have rivalled any of the old-time drivers. At first sight this was not apparent, and the delusion was fostered by a studied carelessness of manner, as though nothing much mattered in this world, plus an ability to run cheerful riot when the occasion fitted. Tough he-men have been known to blench at the tempo and verve of one of Babe's impromptu parties, the pace of which seemed the least fitting training for serious and lengthy races. Yet no man, at any time, could drive further or faster with so little sign of weariness or strain.[163]

> He had not, however, bargained for the competitive spirit of Barnato who, having bought Bentley, wanted to excel – and so far, excelled Bentley had not.

Beneath the nightclub habitué, the companion of starlets and the Gatsby-esque host, W.O recognised, to use a dreadful pun, a driven man like himself. 'His consuming passion in life was to excel', was W.O.'s characteristically laconic and accurate appraisal of the man who bought his motor company.[164]

Having once determined, after careful thought, to take up a sport, he applied himself with religious concentration, starting from the most elementary principles, learning every step by his own experience and dis-regarding all second-hand advice. He once wagered £500 to £100 that he would reduce his golf handicap from seven to scratch in a year, and of course he was successful … What made him such an outstanding driver were his keen eye and judgement, his courage, discretion and self-discipline.[165]

It seems ironic, in view of this assessment of his skills by W.O., that there was initially some disagreement about approaching Barnato with a view to selling him Bentley Motors because he was not thought to be a good enough racing driver.[166] In fact it was probably Barnato's discretion that gave this impression. Although forceful in many aspects of his life, he submitted quite willingly and with great docility to team discipline. As chairman, it would have been easy for him to demand the best car, but in fact the opposite was true, as W.O. related: 'as a driver he regarded himself as an ordinary member of the team, accepting if need be the second string car without demur, and suggesting by his manner and his attitude that it was something of a privilege that he had even been included at all'.[167] As it turned out, Barnato was quite privileged not to have been included in the team that represented Bentley at Le Mans in 1926.

It was not a good summer for Bentley on the track. On 1 June an attempt was made to break the record at Montlhéry in a specially modified and streamlined car. The drivers were Clement, Benjafield, Duller and Barnato. It was going all right until Duller span and came into the pits to find that all the drivers had gone off for a rest. With not even Moir around to take over, a mechanic set off, and crashed after only a third of a lap, almost killing himself. W.O. felt that failure very keenly.

Next was Le Mans. As he had come second the previous year for Sunbeam, Sammy Davis was added to the Bentley team, where he 'felt at once at home, everyone in the team having been a personal friend for quite a long time.'[168] That friendship was to be tested. Three cars were entered; two of them retired, but one – later known as 'Old No.7' – driven by Benjafield and Davis, was still running in the last hour, when, with Sammy at the wheel, it went into a sand-bank and stayed there. The accident cost Bentley a position in the top three; 'despite the kindness of friends, I had let the team down badly after twenty-three and half hours running, and W.O. knew it, which hurt', recalled Davis.[169]

This disaster notwithstanding, Benjy had enjoyed his run at Le Mans,

Barnato at the helm of his powerboat (previous page), *Ardenrun V*, powered by a Bentley engine, racing at Hendon in 1931.

The early stages of the 1926 Le Mans, where all cars were required to run twenty laps of the course with their hoods raised.

becoming sufficiently attached to 'Old No.7' to buy it once it was pulled out of the sandbank. Racing it at Boulogne, the brakes failed and he wrapped it round a tree.

Barnato had not chosen a good year to take over Bentley Motors. W.O. was resigned to giving up racing; the resources of the company would not stand another season and he announced his intention at the next board meeting. He had not, however, bargained for the competitive spirit of Barnato who, having bought Bentley, wanted to excel – and so far, excelled Bentley had not.

> Yes, of course we had given up racing; it was proving too expensive, taking up too much of our time, and we weren't having any luck. We had finished with competition work entirely – but by November we were hard at work preparing the cars for the following June. It was inevitable with Barnato as Chairman, and I had begun to realize the absolute necessity of wiping off those two humiliating defeats. You can't, having once won a race and then failed twice in succession, just lie low and hope that everyone will forget. They don't.[170]

Barnato was as obsessed as Bentley and he had the money ... if Bentley could build the cars and train the drivers. Benjy, in particular, was keen to return and offered his car and his services to the company.

From then on, the Bentley assault on Le Mans took on the complexity of a military manoeuvre. Drivers rehearsed their pit procedure, watched their performance on cine-film and then repeated the process until they could do it blindfolded. Everything was thought of, even down to back-up stopwatches for the timekeepers.

Engineers and mechanics noticed the difference right away: 'we started a proper racing programme for the 1927 season.'[171] 'From our point of view', said another, 'we looked on 1927 as the first real year: we'd sort of played at it before then, with bits and pieces'.[172] A separate racing workshop was established, where proper works cars rather than modified production models were built and tested and race-winning devices such as quick-filling caps and funnels were developed. Barnato was not messing around. He was playing to win, as were Davis and Benjy. 'Benjafield and myself were determined to retrieve our reputations at all costs', recalled Sammy, and it was partly to ensure they would be well prepared that the two men organised the Essex Six Hour Race at Brooklands – a sort of mini-Le Mans, which copied as closely as possible the rules and style of the race mounted by the Automobile Club de l'Ouest.[173]

For Bentley, this race, held at the beginning of May, was to be the first test of the newly invigorated racing *équipe*. What is interesting about this race is that it brought together most of the men who formed the 'Bentley Boys'. Motor racing was an élite pastime with a relatively small coterie of participants and spectators, so all the main personalities would have known

Sammy Davis, taking a bend at high speed, during the 1926 Le Mans.

CHAPTER FOURTEEN

each other. What made the bond between these men so strong was that they would frequently drive one race in a small-engined car of one make and in the next be controlling a far larger car from a different marque altogether. In one race, two drivers might be each other's partners or team-mates, while in the next they could be rivals; these bonds of respect and friendship between the drivers were strong. 'The real joy', in Sammy Davis's opinion, '[was] only realized by the drivers, because for them it is not just the excitement of high speed or lurid incident that counts, but the fact that one's rivals are one's friends.'[174] As close friends, each driver would know the other's character and could gauge what he might be thinking or feeling at any point. Once again, Davis offers a telling insight into the mixed emotions of the British motor racer in the 1920s:

> You see a car fall out and are thankful, maybe, to be rid of a rival, but all the same you realize the bitter disappointment of the driver, know also that what is his fate to-day may be yours to-morrow. In the battle against other cars, temperament comes in. So-and-so is worried if a car keeps just behind him; another friend you know will go 'wild' if his car is passed, and it is fascinating to use this knowledge to help produce the result a team may want.[175]

The men gathered at Brooklands that spring day knew each other very well. Sammy was driving 'a very smart looking 1½-litre four-cylinder Alvis'.[176] Segrave and Duller 'were handling 3-litre Sunbeams'.[177] Dashing Jack Dunfee was piloting a Salmson. As regards Bentleys, Barnato and Benjafield were driving in 'Old No.7', Clement was driving another and Callingham a third. The camaraderie was great; Sammy Davis remembered 'the amount of inter-team leg-pulling being phenomenal'.[178]

That day saw the Bentley début of another keen young sportsman. Captain Henry Ralph Stanley Birkin, known to his friends as 'Tim' (his sister gave him the name after likening him to the cartoon character Tiger Tim), was the thirty-year-old son of a Nottingham baronet whose family had made a fortune in the lace trade. During the First World War he had served, as befitted a Nottingham man, with the 7th Sherwood Foresters and the Royal Warwickshire, before becoming a pilot, spending two years in Palestine. He may have met Barnato out there at the time; certainly the two men had a great deal in common. Both were very rich, both were keen sportsmen (Tim was a crack shot as well as a fast driver) and both were interested in cars. Tim was known to the Bentley brothers as the owner of a D.F.P., which he had raced at Brooklands in 1921.

After that early appearance, not much had been seen of Tim. He had married a baronet's daughter, Audrey Lathan, the same year and promised he would retire from motor racing. They had two daughters and he bought himself Tacolneston Hall, an estate in Norfolk where he enjoyed shooting and farming. Life at Tacolneston was every bit as lively as at Ardenrun. 'I

It was going all right until Duller span and came into the pits to find that all the drivers had gone off for a rest. With not even Moir around to take over, a mechanic set off, and crashed after only a third of a lap, almost killing himself.

used to go duck shooting with him at night, potting at the birds silhouetted against the sky', remembered one houseguest. 'Tacolneston was amazing, and we always used to have lots of fun … Tim would suddenly say "Let's play rugger!": off he'd go, find an old hassock, and there we'd be, charging around the big hall.'[179]

But not everyone at Tacolneston revelled in the Boys' Own lifestyle – Audrey Birkin was far from happy. Tim shared another of Barnato's enthusiasms – women – and his marriage broke down after he was caught in flagrante delicto in a hotel in Blakeney. The Birkins divorced in 1927, leaving Tim free to pursue fast cars and fast women. His friendship with Barnato and his fondness for Bentleys gave the marque a social lustre.

Birkin was intensely shy and prone to melancholia, stammered and was very conscious of his slender build and small stature. As a result of these psychological and physical characteristics, and perhaps not least because of the number of deaths he had seen (including his three siblings), there was a dark streak to him. 'Birkin … was ruthless – with his cars and everybody', was the verdict of one who knew him well and saw him under pressure; however, most of the time Birkin presented a charming, aristocratic exterior.[180]

Typical of his almost heroic insouciance was the way he tells of the occasion he was determined to break the lap record for Brooklands, which at the time stood at 134.2 m.p.h.:

> I was in Le Touquet with Babe Barnato, where he bet me dinner at the Casino that I would not break the record. I flew to Brooklands, where there was a large crowd, and took the car round once to warm it up. After that I tried never to lift my foot from the accelerator; over the bumpy surface, I was once in the air for 40 feet and the car too, but it did two laps of 134.6 and 135.3, and so set up a new record … I flew back to Le Touquet in the evening and had my dinner with Babe.[181]

Tim Birkin, in his distinctive driving ensemble that included a dashing yet potentially hazardous silk scarf.

And he was just as stylish in his appearance as in his gestures. His dress sense was impeccable and young men remarked on his 'uniform' of impeccably cut, checked tweed sports jackets and grey flannel trousers. As a stylish man, Birkin was, of course, friendly with that fashion leader the Prince of Wales, later Duke of Windsor, and he was merely one of the fashionable, Society types Birkin took to visit the Bentley racing workshops.

Birkin's driving ensemble was equally carefully put together, as described by Sammy Davis: 'a dark blue sports shirt, white overall trousers, a distinctive spotted scarf, and a wide belt worn externally, distinguishing him instantly'.[182] Pictures show him lounging nonchalantly around various racetracks; with his hair greased back off his forehead and a little pencil moustache giving him a military mien, he looks more like a guest at a country house party preparing for a game of lawn tennis than a racing driver.

However, according to Tim, the cummerbund was a vital piece of protective clothing. He talked of it as 'a sort of glorified tummy band, which is invaluable; it keeps my inside [sic] together when I am being jolted up and down for hours on end, and in an accident, might prevent the steering wheel from driving into my lungs'.[183]

Like many drivers at the time, Tim was superstitious. Sammy, for instance, drove carrying 'an old silk stocking, with romantic associations', wore headgear modelled on an Iron Age helmet 'he had chanced across in the British Museum years earlier', and had to have a St. Christopher screwed or riveted onto any car he was driving.[184] Tim preferred his St. Christopher in his helmet and he disliked altering his racing attire for similar reasons, even though friends, including Davis, were concerned about the silk scarf he affected while at the wheel. 'That scarf was a constant source of controversy with his friends because, like all its kind, it had a habit of fluttering loose behind his helmet and was then liable to blow suddenly across his goggles.'[185]

He was further distinguished by the habit he developed of sucking oranges while racing.

ON THE ROAD TO GLORY

By dusk, the Bentleys were running so smoothly that you could have set your watch by the progress of the 4½-litre car as it roared round the course.

CHAPTER FOURTEEN

Birkin at speed, at Brooklands in one of his supercharged Blower Bentleys.

A photograph shows him turning a corner, a citrus fruit locked between his jaws, giving a good impression of a suckling pig. Anyone who drove as his partner would find the floor of the car littered with oranges that had been sucked dry and then dropped on the floor, where they would shrivel up and turn black due to the heat generated during a race.

Although Tim was conscious he was not very tall and that he stammered, it seemed women found the combination of his looks, aristocratic bearing, money, clothes, dare-devil insouciance and stammer hard to resist.

He turned up for the Essex Six Hours with his 22-year-old brother Charles Archibald Birkin. Tim and Archie had both bought Bentleys at the end of 1925 and Tim had bought a new one in February 1927, perhaps to celebrate his divorce. It was in this car that he appeared at Brooklands.

For all their preparation, the Works Bentleys did not fare at all well. Although the carefully drilled pit work and the time it took the drivers to raise and lower the hoods were exemplary, the new duralumin rockers, with which the team cars had been equipped, began to break up during the race.

However, despite some truly wild and erratic driving from Archie, who was quickly removed, Tim Birkin kept going, letting Frank Clement share the drive when his team car retired, and they managed to bring the privately owned Bentley into third place on distance and eighth on handicap, broken gearbox notwithstanding. A bad result, but had it not been for Birkin it would have been worse. It is a gloomy postscript to this race that Archie died a little later that year while practising for a motorcycle race.

Barnato had been due to drive at Le Mans, but business kept him in London that June. It is interesting to speculate whether that business meeting was really so crucial that he had to miss his Le Mans début, or whether, as a man addicted to winning, he was afraid of losing face as both racing driver and company chairman, should a mechanical fault, such as a faulty duralumin rocker, force his retirement from the race.

Preparation continued with an almost manic fervour. W.O. was loath to let anything slip out of his control. He wanted to pair Sammy with Clement in an experimental car, a 4½-litre that went by the evocative moniker of 'Old Mother Gun'. The new car would have given Sammy an advantage, but being sentimental, honourable and romantic, he refused to be split from Benjy and 'Old No.7' – he felt he owed both the doctor and his 3-litre and insisted on driving with them. W.O. relented, but, doubtless keen to avoid the sort of disagreement he had had with Duff in the Le Mans pits in 1925, he insisted 'Old No.7' be returned to Bentley for the period of the race and be treated as a works car, with both vehicle and drivers remaining under his total control.

The Bentley team appeared at the Hôtel Moderne in Le Mans a week before the race and immediately began training; the weather was hot and the team practised using five-gallon milk churns for refuelling, which took some getting used to, drenching Benjy in the process and causing him to

> Some time after half past nine something happened: the 4½ was late.

The Bentley pit counter, a bank of apprehensive faces, including a pensive-looking W.O. at the back, during the 1927 Le Mans.

remove his upper garments – much to the ribaldry of the onlookers. Benjy was, as usual, the butt of many jokes, and George Duller was the instigator of one of the better ones. The jockey called the doctor over from where he was enjoying a drink, ostensibly to help lift a cylinder block from a car.

> Arriving, he was given the rope, told to mount the ladder, which he did, told to put the rope over a beam, which he did, told to make a noose in the end of the rope, which he did. So far Benjy was naturally convinced that he was helping us to get ready to replace the damaged car's cylinder block. Then George, with an expression a graven image would have envied, said to Benjy, "Now put the loop round your neck and jump off." For a moment it looked as though "our bald-headed chemist", as Clement called him … would do the thing, then he whizzed down the ladder and we had much ado to preserve George's existence.[186]

In fact it was only Clement calling for some wheel-changing practice that brought things under control, leaving the two men too tired to fight.

That was the way of Bentley preparation at Le Mans. Often drivers were up before dawn, 'suffering greatly from liver', even though 'naturally the team as a whole lived a life as "dry" as any eccentric American reformer would wish'.[187] However accidents will happen: one afternoon the team got so bad tempered on some sticky dark brown spirit that they were led to bed, but they unlocked their connecting doors and continued to argue until late into the night.

On the day of the race, with Barnato absent on business, the line up was Benjy and Sammy in 'Old No. 7', Clement and Callingham in the 4½ and Duller driving the other 3-litre with Baron d'Erlanger. This last pairing was sheer, if unintentional, genius: Duller the irreverent prankster was paired with a sardonic financier and playboy whose imperturbable countenance concealed a sense of humour as arid as the Sahara. Whether W.O. appreciated the wit of this pairing is not known.

By dusk, the Bentleys were running so smoothly that you could have set your watch by the progress of the 4½-litre car as it roared round the course. Six minutes after it had last been seen from the pits, the hum of its engine could be heard distantly at Arnage; two minutes after that its headlamps could be seen and eight minutes and 45 seconds after it had last passed the pits, 'Old Mother Gun' would thunder past and into the darkness once more…

Then some time after half past nine something happened: the 4½ was late. Reluctant to tell W.O., the timekeeper eventually turned, to see W.O.'s face ash-white – he knew to the second when to expect 'Old Mother Gun' and she was long overdue. But then it was the same all along the pit lane; not one of the 22 cars that had entered the race could be heard or seen. For the first time at Le Mans that day, the croaking of frogs could be heard …

Chapter Fifteen

It was 9.30 at night on Saturday 18 June and Sammy Davis was at the wheel of Old No.7, coming downhill to the White House Corner at Le Mans.

He noticed a small amount of debris in the road and slowed from 100 m.p.h. to around 80;

it was probably nothing, but given his guilty conscience after the previous year's disaster in the final hour, the last thing he wanted to do was to repeat the mistake and have to face the silent fury of W.O.'s piercing gaze.

> As the car swung round the White House corner, his headlamps picked up a barrier of twisted metal.

What he saw when he turned the corner was to become one of motor racing's most celebrated and oft-told stories, one that Sammy himself would recount many times over the next half century. However, just then it was the next few seconds that concerned him. As the car swung round the White House corner, his headlamps picked up a barrier of twisted metal. Three cars had crashed. Two of them were Bentleys.

Callingham had come round the corner in the 4½, found a car across his path, swerved to avoid it, but failed to stay on the road, rolling the car and half blocking the road. Duller was next to join the pile up, missing the first French car, but smashing into the 4½-litre and finishing up on top of it. Duller's training as a jockey probably saved his life as he jumped clear of the wreckage just before the impact. Sammy was round the corner and, although he had slowed fractionally, he slid sideways into the Bentley sandwich at the roadside, raising his arm to shield himself from the vehicles he thought would topple onto him. He described the noise as the 'rending crash of riven metal'[188] or 'a lot of dustbins falling off a roof.'[189]

He got out of the car and looked frantically through the wreckage for his team-mates, only to get a shock when he turned to find Duller behind him, bleeding but not seriously hurt. Callingham too was uninjured. Relieved, Sammy's thoughts returned to the race. He managed to restart his car and reversed it from the wreckage of the rest of his team, the car disentangling itself with more rending and screeching. He drove away moments before another car slammed into the wreckage. Including 'Old No.7', seven cars were involved in the pile-up, but only one driver, the first to crash, was seriously hurt. Sammy nursed the stricken car back to the pits, all the time turning over in his mind what he might have done instead and how he would face W.O.

Back at the pits he worked like a maniac. The front of the car – axle, frame, cross-member, mudguard, one front wheel … the lot – was distorted. Only one headlamp could be made to work; the battery dangled off the running board and had to be tied into place; the brakes were not all they might be but 'could be controlled' and, although there was steering, it was 'odd and without return action.'[190] However, the 'engine fired at once' and, ignoring the entreaties of his team, Sammy set off, determined to finish. 'Of course, to win was hopeless now.'[191]

Eighteen hours later, he crossed the finish line, having covered 1472.527 miles at an average speed of 61.354 m.p.h. The second-placed car was more than 200 miles behind them. Driving a wrecked car that only a madman – or a man suffering from shock and too scared to admit defeat to W.O. – would have even dared to start up, Sammy and the bald-headed chemist had won Le Mans in the most spectacular circumstances.

After the crash, it had rained so hard that one driver had even stopped and erected his hood, but all the time Sammy and Benjy had gained steadily

The notorious White House crash (previous page) of the 1927 Le Mans, the Bentley 3 Litre of Duller and d'Erlanger lies in the ditch. To deter looters, a mechanic was left to guard the car.

The victory dinner for the 1927 Le Mans, held at the Savoy five days after the race. The guest of honour was 'Old No. 7' who was hoisted into the hotel's dining room.

on the leader. Shortly before noon, W.O. heard a change in the engine note of the leading car and ordered the Bentley to put the pressure on. Benjy, who was driving the wounded car flat out, its mudguard flapping like a broken wing, manfully obeyed. He overtook the leader just as it retired with engine trouble.

Shortly before the end of the race, Benjy made an unscheduled pit stop and got out, insisting that Sammy be the driver to cross the finishing line. What had seemed like a routine race turned into a disaster, and then became a very British – and very Bentley – triumph.

The effect was electric. The motoring press lapped up the drama. According to *The Motor*, 'Even the "Paris-Madrid" – the race which is a classic so far as the number of crashes is concerned – never produced such an amazing sequence of events as last Saturday's and Sunday's 24-hour race at Le Mans.'[192] *The Autocar*, too, invoked the Paris-Madrid, and went on to claim that the race was 'marked by acts of chivalry and good breeding only too often unhappily absent from so-called sporting events today'.[193]

Nor was it just the motoring press that got excited. The *Daily Mail* ran a leading article that concluded that the victory 'serves to point the truth that there are no cars in the world to equal those of British manufacture in the quality and strength of both engine and chassis'.[194]

Captain Wilfred Gordon Aston captured the mood of patriotism in the *Tatler* at the end of the month when he wrote, 'I'll bet there isn't a single British motorist, irrespective of the sort of car he owns, and whether or not he has ever been in a Bentley, who did not feel delighted that the

Bentley had run to conspicuous victory in the great twenty-four hours' race at Le Mans.'[195]

The Friday following the team's return to London, *The Autocar* hosted a dinner at the Savoy to celebrate Bentley's impressive achievement. This outstanding victory was going to be milked for all the publicity it was worth. It reflected well on everyone. *The Autocar* was pleased because the winning driver was one of its correspondents, and it invited the suppliers and supporters of the Bentley team along to share the feeling of participation in this epic feat, where victory had been plucked from the jaws of the White House crash.

During the dinner – a truly formal affair with all the men in white tie – the host, Sir Edward Iliffe C.B.E. M.P., rose to announce that 'a lady who was entitled to be at dinner was outside, adding that he had invited her to enter. At that, folding doors swung back, there was a fine roar of engine, and, with her one headlamp blazing, number "Seven" came into the room.'[196] Sammy and Benjy were greatly moved and it is fitting that the two kindest, most generous-spirited of the Bentley Boys would be the ones to restore the company to the winner's podium.

However, the line between the shame of the preceding year and the glory of 1927 was a fine one and Sammy's contrasting experiences were put to use some years later when he published a small folio of his cartoons. In one of them he depicts two racing drivers: one has a halo, wings and victor's laurels and is seated on sacks of prize money hoisting aloft a goblet

Experience suggests that you may be regarded as this if you win—

but you will certainly be regarded as this if you lose.

of Champagne; the other, a man with a fist replaced by a ham and a tail signifying his infernal status, is seen walking away from a pile of bills. 'Experience suggests that you may be regarded as this if you win', runs the caption over the angelic character, while the picture of the demonic ham-fisted loser appears with the caption 'but you will certainly be regarded as this if you lose'.[197]

For the moment Benjy and Sammy were enjoying the fruits of victory.

The following Wednesday, Bentley Motors gave a dinner to mark the victory and on Friday the R.A.C. organised a celebratory lunch. All the while, 'shoals of letters and telegrams from all over the country' expressed the enthusiasm of what was seen as a British victory, albeit one made possible by the single-minded men of Bentley Motors.[198]

There is also a revealing postscript to the Le Mans victory of 1927. Barnato wanted to show his appreciation of the victory and asked Benjy if there was anything that he wanted. None of the Bentley Boys, with the exception of Clement, was particularly interested in racing for money, so Benjy replied with typical flippancy, "Oh well, a million. But as you probably haven't got it, then something for my hospital."[199] Benjy promptly forgot all about it. 'Months later, Babe asked Benjy to lunch, and had difficulty in getting him to accept since Benjy said that he was a very busy man. After that lunch was over Babe handed over cheques for very large amounts for both of Benjy's hospitals.'[200] It is a shame that, while Barnato's reluctance to lend money or offer a cigarette is frequently mentioned, this incident – and perhaps other examples of his disinterested generosity and philanthropy – is little known.

Sammy Davis's Casques cartoons (opposite) depicting the bitter-sweet life of a motor racing driver.

'Old No. 7' as guest of honour at the celebratory Bentley dinner following the team's win at the 1927 Le Mans.

PART FOUR

The golden years

Chapter Sixteen

The rest of the 1920s were effectively the golden years of Bentley. With Barnato's money, W.O.'s engineering skills and the superb publicity gained by Sammy and Benjy, Bentley became le dernier cri. After the victory at Le Mans in 1927 everyone suddenly wanted to be part of the Bentley story: the marque commanded the attention of rich sportsmen in particular, who thirsted for the romance and glory of the racetrack.

THE GOLDEN YEARS

1929.
LE MANS. Drivers of the four Bentleys :- D'Erlanger, Barnato, Birkin, Jack Dunfee, Kidston, Benjafield, Chassagne, And Clement.

CHAPTER SIXTEEN

It is safe to say that Bentley's Le Mans success captured the imagination of the nation. Had the race been as uneventful as it had initially seemed, and had the Bentleys taken the flag in first, second and third place, as looked possible, would the 1927 victory have had such an impact? Probably not. It was the drama of the circumstances, the pluck of the drivers, and the fact that a British team had come back from near-certain defeat to see off competition from all over the world that shaped the Bentley image.

After this result, a myth grew up around the marque. Consequently, at the Essex Six Hour race of 1928, another rich young man joined the cadre of rake-hells who had taken up the fashionable pastime of racing Bentleys. Bernard Rubin, partnering Benjy in a 4½-litre, was a 31-year-old Australian, whose father, Mark Rubinstein, had emigrated from Lithuania to Australia in the 1880s, where he did with pearls what Barney Barnato had done with diamonds in South Africa.

Badly wounded during the war, Rubin was unable to walk when he inherited his father's fortune at the tender age of 22. Recovering, he became interested in motor racing after meeting Barnato. Naturally, the two became friends, and it is part of Bentley lore that Rubin and Barnato, as well as Birkin, all had flats in the southeast corner of Grosvenor Square, which became known as Bentley's Corner.[201]

The fourth Bentley Boy to live at Bentley's Corner was still in his twenties. Commander Glen Kidston R.N. was the scion of a wealthy shipbuilding dynasty that had made its money in the shipyards of the Clyde. In many ways he was another version of Birkin: rich and well-connected – Dickie Mountbatten was typical of his circle – he was fond of field sports and fascinated by the speed of the increasingly well-engineered cars of the 1920s.

As a boy, Kidston had been passionate about the outdoor life of the landed classes. His letters home from school ask how many stags and grouse his father had shot and pleaded with his mother to send him the white heather of his beloved Scottish moors. His was an eventful life. He attended Royal Naval College, Osborne, on the Isle of Wight, and then Dartmouth, and as a young teenager found himself a midshipman on *H.M.S. Hogue*, which was sunk in the battle of Heligoland Bight in 1914. He was picked up by a Dutch vessel, only to be given a tot of rum and thrown back into the water to make room for the wounded.

On his return to Britain, Kidston joined the submarine service and got into other scrapes, including being stuck on the ocean floor in the world's largest submarine. He raced motorcycles – he even had one on his submarine – shot, fished, hunted big game in Africa, boxed and became interested in cars, owning various makes and models, including, of course, a couple of Bentleys. However, it was at the wheel of a Bugatti that he first achieved fame in motoring circles, putting up a good performance at the

> Bentley's Le Mans success captured the imagination of the nation.

4½ Litre Bentleys at the 1928 Le Mans (previous page), cornering sharply at Pontlieue. The hazardous hairpin bend was removed from the Le Mans course in 1929.

The winning Bentley team and cars (opposite, above) for the 1929 Le Mans, taking the top four positions.

The victorious drivers for the 1929 Le Mans (opposite, below), from left to right: d'Erlanger, Barnato, Birkin, Dunfee, Kidston, Benjafield, Chassagne and Clement.

THE GOLDEN YEARS

> These men were hedonists, who enjoyed and indulged themselves.

Kidston and Barnato, with their winners' bouquets, enjoying a post-race cigarette.

1925 Grand Prix de Provence and being the first person to race the new 2-litre Grand Prix Bugatti at Brooklands.

Like Birkin, Kidston married a debutante, the bewitchingly beautiful Nancy Soames, and, again like Birkin, promised that he would give up motor racing. He sold his Grand Prix Bugatti – which looked like a go-kart next to his Bentley – to George Duller. Although Nancy bore him a son, Archie, their marriage was not a happy one. Inevitably, as his marriage deteriorated, his love of motor racing bloomed again, just as Birkin's had.

Kidston, again like Birkin, was a patriot – an unfashionable word today, but something that was part of the sportsman's psychological make-up in those days. These were men who had fought the 'war to end all wars' and, though they lived well and did not have to work, they felt an obligation to their country. This was not the hackneyed desire 'to give something back to society' that afflicts so many of today's fleeting celebrities, who, feeling their fame on the wane, devote themselves to self-consciously charitable works – far from it. These men were hedonists, who enjoyed and indulged themselves, unsentimental in many ways but also capable of feeling a strong sense of national duty and pride. And in a way, it was this exaggerated sense of duty, this desire to excel for their country, that would kill both men before they were out of their thirties. It is not too much to say that they really did believe Britain was a land fit for heroes and, as they saw it, it was their responsibility to provide the heroism.

Le Mans, naturally, was where the Bentley Boys liked to demonstrate their heroics. The 24-hour race of 1928 offered another dramatic victory for the Bentley team, which now included Tim Birkin, partnered with Jean

Chassagne (who had driven the car against which 'Old No. 7' had competed and won towards the end of the previous year's Le Mans). Benjy was back, this time paired with Clement in a 4½-litre, and Barnato, who drove with Bernard Rubin.

The Le Mans of 1928 was a swashbuckling *Boys' Own* affair that stirred the nation. From the start, lap records fell to the Bentleys and their chief rival that year, the Stutzes. Birkin's car blew a tyre, which wrapped itself around the brake drum, taking 90 minutes to free. Instead of piloting the car back to the pits at a sensible speed, Birkin tried to get away with going 'well over' 70 m.p.h.[202] Inevitably, his wheel buckled, leaving him to run the remaining three miles, after which his co-driver Chassagne shouldered a pair of jacks and jogged off to do his best to re-enter the race. In all, the delay cost three hours. Before dawn, Benjy and Clement were out with a cracked chassis and Barnato managed to win by only a narrow margin; with four laps to go, his chassis cracked too, detaching the radiator hose so that the car was overheating badly for the last few laps.

This time the victory dinner was at the Lyons Corner House and the menu bore a cartoon of Barnato being chased by the Stutz. Four hundred guests were present and although there was musical entertainment laid on, it was ignored in the stampede to get autographs. Barnato adored the attention and his celebrity status even landed him a role endorsing a brand of cigarettes.

"He loved having his photo taken and all the rest of it", was the way it was seen from the factory floor and the pits. "Barnato loved his racing, there's no doubt of that. And he loved to win and to be in the limelight – but he was a good sport if anyone beat him – though that didn't happen often."[203]

Every time the British racing-green Bentleys appeared at the start of a race, it was almost axiomatic that they would win. Le Mans of 1929 was little more than a procession of the Bentleys around Le Circuit de La Sarthe, with the winged 'B' taking first, second, third and fourth places. W.O. did not believe in driving his cars any faster than was needed to win a race and thus it was that the 1929 Le Mans was running so slowly that Jack Dunfee, who was paired with Kidston, actually got out and had a drink at the Café de l'Hippodrome. Indeed, he was so frustrated at the low speeds he was being asked to maintain that he asked a rather impertinent question: "I say, W.O., do you want me to get out and push the ruddy thing?"[204]

Of course no employee of Bentley Motors would have dared talk to W.O. like that – and it is difficult to imagine many of the other drivers using such a tone – but Dunfee was not an employee and nor, probably, was he that bothered what went on under the bonnet of the cars he drove. Like the other Bentley Boys, he was a gentleman racing for pleasure and his casual, flippant insouciance played well with the newspapers, the pretty girls and the rest of the Bentley Boys, among whom his role was that of

***The start of the 1928 Le Mans**, with Birkin's 4½ Litre leading Clement and Barnato.*

> His casual, flippant insouciance played well with the newspapers, the pretty girls and the rest of the Bentley Boys.

Barnato looks down on Kidston, who is working on their car in the Bentley pits during the 1929 Le Mans. The rules of Le Mans precluded anyone but the driver working on the car.

class clown. As Birkin recalled:

> We were always seen together; we had the same manner of speech, the same jokes among ourselves. Jack Dunfee was our official jester; it was he who invented the 'School'. W.O. was its headmaster; a car was a satchel, and petrol was ink; Jack Dunfee turned every incident into something to do with the 'School', and talked about it in an appalling drawl.[205]

However, this silliness was a cause of some friction in the pits. The class system of Great Britain was faithfully reproduced in the microcosm of Bentley Motors and there were tensions between the mechanics and the racing drivers. Although Bentley employed middle-class and even aristocratic young men in his workshops – Lord Settrington, later Duke of Richmond and Gordon, started his adult life as a mechanic at Bentley – they tended to be the exception, and there was a sense of resentment at the glory enjoyed by the Bentley Boys.

Of all Bentley employees, Frank Clement had the most reason to feel a little put out. "They were great fun", he once said of the Bentley Boys, "but some of them could be a nuisance at times". As far as Clement was concerned, it was the ignorance of the machinery they were driving that was the biggest irritation. "It was the drivers' lack of mechanical knowledge and workshop techniques that was the worst. It did matter, I felt, and it was very awkward sometimes, especially at Le Mans." The rules at that time precluded anyone but the driver working on the car, so "if something went wrong on my car that the driver could not do, it meant that I had to be fetched out from my rest – usually in the middle of the night – and that meant I had to drive again. I had several doses of that", he recalled, a trifle bitterly. "Benjy was fine, except he had no idea at all on mechanics – absolutely none. Then I had George Duller: he was very, very nice, but, again, not a mechanic of any kind." Kidston "was a nice chap, though he would not obey orders". And as for Birkin, whom Clement called a "lone wolf" and a "car-wrecker", "Not for anything would I have ridden in a race with Birkin."[206]

What also annoyed Clement was the high-handed attitude, perhaps quite unconscious, of the amateur drivers, who would "want something done at the last minute before the race and take away your pet mechanic - that rather spoilt it". The real difficulty was that they were accountable to no one. "Of course, we had no hold on them; I suppose that was the real problem. But then they did have great publicity value – the best ones did, anyway."[207] Hardly a ringing endorsement.

And while the publicity value, not to mention the fact they drove for fun, helped the firm, even W.O. had to put up with some fairly salty words: when the lights kept going out on his Bentley in one race, Jack Dunfee pulled into the pits to give W.O. a dressing down: "it was the first time I'd ever heard anybody really get angry with W.O. He said some rude words

over the counter, did Jack", recalls one who saw the altercation.²⁰⁸ Kidston had a reputation as a man who "upset everybody … but likeable all the same".²⁰⁹ Another mechanic describes Kidston as "the only naval officer I had to shout at".²¹⁰ The same mechanic was also tempted to have a go at Birkin for his behaviour during pit stops. "When he filled up, the tanks and cans used to come flying back in the pits like cannon-balls. I often felt like shying them back at him."²¹¹

And then there was the legendary Champagne lifestyle, which was a reality. Sammy Davis describes the method by which flagging drivers were revived: 'well swizzled champagne and water inside, with Eau de Cologne and water externally.'²¹² Wally Hassan flatly refused to ride as a mechanic with Rubin in the thrill-packed Irish T.T. of 1929; 'he was a shocker', came the bald verdict, "I refused to ride with him because I had a shrewd idea he'd be pickled".²¹³

'I refused to ride with him because I had a shrewd idea he'd be pickled.'

THE GOLDEN YEARS

The start of the 1929 Le Mans (top); Bentleys went on to take 1st, 2nd, 3rd and 4th positions.

Birkin's Bentley Speed Six (above) powers along at the 1929 Le Mans.

Indeed, the sparkling wines of Epernay and the Marne were an integral part of the pre-, during and post-racing rhythm of motor sport in those less health-and-safety-conscious times. Saunders strikes an air that is part dismissive, part wide-eyed, at the style of living that was considered completely normal by the Bentley Boys:

> I mean, we knew most of them were playboys and that. And the way they fixed themselves up at Le Mans – the pit they used was just like a small hotel – it was a revelation. They'd have all the wine, champagne, eats, chickens, and everything that went with it. They'd have the head chauffeurs, butlers, secretaries and heaven knows what – hangers-on too, plenty of them and the womenfolk – some beautiful women, too.[214]

Ah yes, the women. When they weren't chasing glory on the track, the Bentley Boys were chasing skirt, a pastime that often spilled out of the bedroom and into the pit lane. For instance, in 1926, while the team were on the way to Montlhéry, havoc was caused in Paris with one member of the Bentley party having to be bailed out, first from a brothel where he refused to pay his bill and then later from the *Gendarmerie*.

Women were always bound to be drawn to the Bentley Boys, whose perceived minimum membership requirements were money, social prominence, looks, availability and an overall *carpe diem* attitude to life. Indeed, it seems that such was the appetite of the more ambitious ones that they would finish with one Bentley Boy and then move on to another. 'On three occasions', remembered W.O. Bentley in later life, 'I was begged by three different drivers to meet "the most wonderful woman you've ever met, W.O.", and each time it was the same "wonderful woman". 'We knew

CHAPTER SIXTEEN

each other pretty well by coffee at the end of the third meal', concluded Bentley wryly.²¹⁵

It was one thing for women to be hanging around the drivers' bedrooms, but it was another matter entirely when they started draping themselves decoratively around the Bentley pits. Apparently it was Birkin who was the real problem: "quite a lady's man", was the polite way one observer put it.²¹⁶ And by the 1929 Le Mans W.O. felt it was time to set a few ground rules. As ever, he was the essence of brevity: "no one in the pit – you understand, no one except those authorized to be here", he said to Clarke, his pit manager. "There's plenty of room next door for them." Everyone knew to whom he was referring.

And for a while it went well enough; a couple of changes of driver had been effected and night was falling when W.O. looked up to see two women in the pit. He looked over at his pit manager. "Who are they?". Clarke shook his head in ignorance. "Turn them out", came the peremptory instruction from W.O. The pit manager walked towards the two women. "Excuse me ... but ladies are not allowed in this pit; this is the working pit. Would you mind withdrawing next door?" [This was either *The Autocar* pit or the sponsored pit for drivers, both noted for their lavish hospitality.] "Oh", came the cut-glass accent, "but we are with Sir Henry."²¹⁷ "Look", said an un-amused pit manager, "you can be with the devil himself, but our god in the corner there has spoken. To please him – please ... go ... out. Otherwise I've got orders to put you out."²¹⁸ One of the women turned out to be Birkin's sister, but instead of causing a scene, pointless in the face of W.O.'s monosyllabic implacability, the two women withdrew to the much

When they weren't chasing glory on the track, the Bentley Boys were chasing skirt.

THE GOLDEN YEARS

The invitation to Barnato's post-Le Mans party (above), thrown to celebrate the win in 1929.

Barnato and Kidston, larking about with a mocked up Bentley go-kart **(opposite). Where this picture was taken is not known but a press cutting from December 1929 shows an identical go-kart decorated with Kidston's photo and a sign that reads 'This car is powered with a Damwell Killus Supercharger'. Numerous famous racing drivers, including Barnato and Birkin took part in the 1929 'Grand Prix de Berkley Square' during the Shell-Mex Ball at the Mayfair Hotel – a race in toy motor cars that comprised of 'two laps of Mayfair Cocktail and Caberet Circuit'.**

more convivial pit next door, and a few days afterwards Clarke was sent a very handsome wallet for his handling of the situation.

The victory party at Le Mans that year more than made up for the absence of excitement on the circuit and the lack of diverting female companionship in the working pit. It was a lavish, typically Barnato affair that made great use of Ardenrun and its drive. The invitation and the care with which the evening was planned showed just how much Barnato revelled in the achievements of his company.

Poor old Benjy – always the butt of the Bentley Boys' jokes, but then as the only one with a serious, useful job, it was probably inevitable that he would be ragged. Anyway, like everything in the gilded existence of the Bentley Boys, it was just good fun. And on that Sunday morning, as the flappers and show-business people who were such a part of Barnato's parties went to bed, and as the sun came up over Ardenrun, catching an empty Champagne bottle here and there in the dewy grass, life must indeed have seemed great fun: one long party with pretty girls, fast cars and the time and money to indulge them.

Yet just a few months later, on 24 October 1929, the bubble of prosperity and wellbeing that encased the decade-long party known as the 'Roaring Twenties' finally burst. The stock market on Wall Street collapsed. By noon, police riot squads were needed to control crowds in the city's financial district and, despite intervention by New York's leading bankers to support the market, the sustained run of good fortune and prosperity was over. Eleven financiers committed suicide that very day and many more would follow their example.

CHAPTER SIXTEEN

Life must indeed have seemed great fun: one long party with pretty girls, fast cars and the time and money to indulge them.

Chapter Seventeen

before we leave the twenties and the girls behind,

it is interesting to look at two women, each very different from the other, yet each representative of the emancipated women of the age.

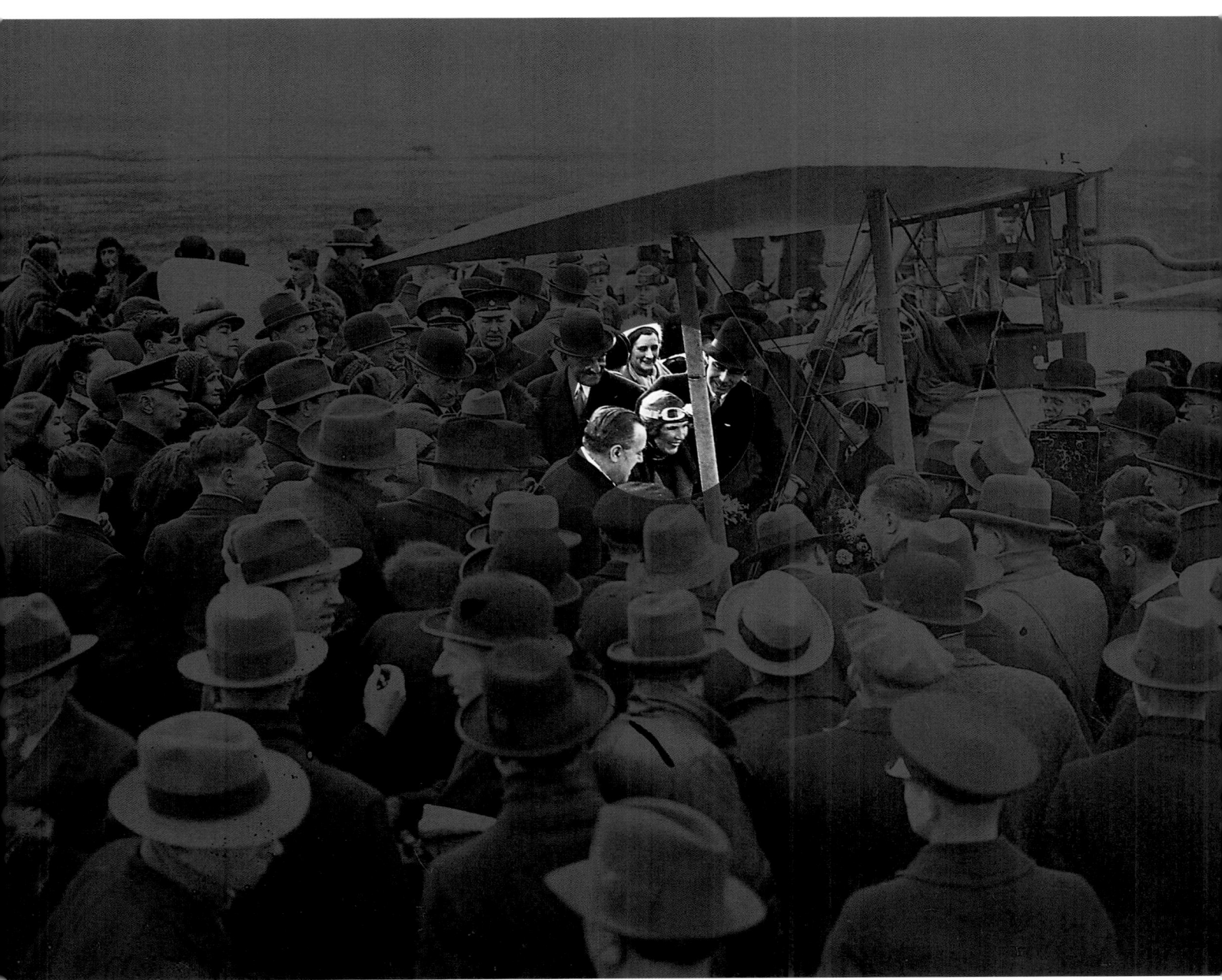

On her return to Croydon Aerodrome, a crowd surges around the Hon. Mrs Victor Bruce (previous page) following her solo flight around the world in February 1931.

The Hon. Mrs Victor Bruce, a remarkable and glamorous women, at Montlhéry in 1929 driving 24 hours solo at over 89 m.p.h. in a 4½ Litre Bentley to set a Class C record.

The social position of women had changed: a generation earlier, women sacrificed their liberty – and, in one case at least, their lives – to enjoy the right to vote.[219] During the First World War, women had taken jobs on the Home Front, and after the war many of them wanted to enjoy civilian life to the full. For the Hon. Mrs Victor Bruce, that meant the thrill of driving the latest sports and racing cars to the limit of their performance. Attitudes towards women drivers were changing too. In June 1927 Brooklands held its first motor race for women, in which the recently married Hon. Mrs Victor Bruce drove a stylish A.C. in cream and aluminium.

Pictures of the time show a poised and glamorous beauty; she was by any standards a remarkable woman and in the years following the First World War, must have seemed extraordinary. Mary Petre was born into the landed gentry – her father was squire of Coptfold Hall, Essex – in 1895 and married the Hon. Victor Austin Bruce in 1926, just after he had won the Monte Carlo Rally. Her husband shared her sense of adventure and did not mind being upstaged by a woman who raced boats as well as cars and dabbled in record-breaking aviation, too. Once, while his wife was flying solo round the world, a reporter remarked that Bruce had to be a "funny sort of chap to allow [his] wife to fly round the world on her own". Yes, agreed Bruce, it was rather amusing. "The very idea of my letting her do anything is humorous. When she makes up her mind to do something she just goes ahead and does it without taking notice of anyone."[220]

In the late spring of 1929 Mary made up her mind to break the record for 'single-handed driving for twenty-four hours', a feat best attempted at Montlhéry. She was no stranger to the oval track outside Paris: in 1927 she and Victor had attempted a ten-day endurance run there, but Victor had rolled the A.C. after covering 15,000 miles in 147 hours. However, she was told that the car 'could not be hotted up any further', which came as a blow, for she was very attached to her sporty little car.[221]

Her memoirs have an agreeably brisk 'jolly hockey-sticks' indomitableness and heartiness. 'I began wracking my brains to find another car which would go fast enough, long enough; over breakfast one morning the answer popped into my head – the 4½-litre Bentley!' It was a brainwave that put an end to all thoughts of toast, marmalade and Darjeeling. 'Without finishing my breakfast, I telephoned the Bentley Company and made an appointment with W.O. Bentley himself.' Although she says that W.O. 'agreed readily', it is unlikely that she would have allowed any disagreement on W.O.'s part to stand in her way.

'Don't call me a women's libber!'

When she turned up the following day, she found the taciturn W.O. had enlisted the moral support of Barnato, who was doubtless curious to meet this feisty and very attractive woman. She was characteristically direct. 'Briskly I told them that I wanted to borrow one of their cars, why I wanted it, and where I was going to take it.' W.O. was just as straightforward. "We've only one car available – Tim Birkin's mount. He's driving in several international races this year and Earl Howe is to drive it in the twenty-four hour race at Le Mans next month."

But she was not a woman to let a little thing like the competition schedule of Britain's most famous racing driver stand in the way of her record attempt. "That twenty-four hour run at Montlhéry will run it in beautifully for them. I hope to average at least a hundred miles an hour, which means I'll need a car that can be hotted up to do about a hundred and seven." "Who's your co-driver?", W.O. asked. "I've no co-driver", came the reply. "I'm going alone."

Barnato was not happy and the look he gave W.O. showed his feelings plainly enough, but W.O. was intrigued and, in the spirit of Professor Higgins, he said, "I believe she might do it."[222] Indeed, she must have caught W.O. on a very good morning because, as well as letting her borrow Birkin's car, he offered to pay for the shipping of the vehicle and the mechanics to work on it.

Her car arranged, she booked the circuit for 6 and 7 June, squeezed some sponsorship out of Dunlop then, to celebrate, she went shopping. 'I went to Bond Street and bought myself a pale blue leather jacket for the occasion. It had no special padding, but I thought it looked very smart. Throughout my racing career I never wore any special kit. I was never keen on overalls or slacks, but always drove in a blouse, tailored skirt and string of pearls.'[223] Her delight in pushing cars to their limits did not mean that she sacrificed her sense of style. "Don't call me a woman's libber!", she said crisply to one interviewer. "I don't approve of that sort of thing. I was a girl among five brothers and I have always tried to remain feminine."[224]

The time of the record attempt drew near and, to add a little more excitement to the proceedings, the mechanics driving the car over to France were accompanied by a representative from Shell, who wanted to drive the car himself. Unfortunately, he lost control in the wet, hitting a tree and sending one mechanic over the windscreen. Once the car had been disentangled from the tree and dragged up a 15-foot banking back onto the road, they discovered the front axle had been bent by the frame buckling. One of them recalled a Boulogne garage that was familiar with Bentleys and, once there, phoned the Bentley works to get an axle shipped over straight away. Once they knew it was going to be alright, the man from the oil company took the mechanics out for a dinner, after which they worked their way through the shelf of spirits and *digestifs* and enjoyed a post-prandial 'argument with some gendarmes' before turning in for the night. "It was just as well the axle didn't arrive any earlier than twelve o'clock", recalled one of the revellers ruefully, "because I was certainly a bit rough in the morning".[225]

Despite hangovers and the sort of damage that, but for some quick thinking, could have written off the car and the record attempt, the Bentley was waiting for the Hon. Mrs Bruce at Montlhéry. She herself had had a somewhat hair-raising journey to the circuit; her taxi driver, like his counterpart at Le Mans a few years earlier, had felt obliged to demonstrate his high-speed motoring skills. Mrs Bruce knew something was up when the driver 'whipped off his beret, fumbled in the dashboard pocket and pulled out a white flying helmet'.[226] When at last she stumbled, dazed, out of the taxi at the track, the driver tried to refuse payment on the grounds that it had been an honour to drive her, but, weakly muttering thanks and expressing her praise, she pressed the money into his hand and felt quite relieved to be driving herself for the next 24 hours. 'I have made many adventurous journeys on land, sea, and air, but that taxi trip to Montlhéry on that June morning I shall always remember', she later wrote.[227]

Bringing style to the racetrack, the achievements of the Hon. Mrs Victor Bruce are equal to any Bentley Boy.

At the circuit, the conditions were not encouraging. Drizzle had made the track slippery and there was one other small problem that everyone had overlooked – Mrs Bruce, used to the compact A.C., could barely see over the dashboard of the Bentley and had trouble reaching the pedals. Some cushions were fetched from the timekeeper's hut and the necessary adjustments were made, enabling her to operate the pedals and see where she was going. Nevertheless, it was a good idea that she was not intending to use the handbrake: she would have needed to stand up to get hold of this lever on the outside of the car. After a practice lap, during which she noticed that the shock absorbers were screwed down so tight that every bump battered her shoulders and impeded her breathing, there was just time for a nice cup of tea before she set off in heavy rain at midday.

Twenty-four hours later, having almost fallen asleep at one critical point and having taken a swig from a bottle of petrol that she mistook for water, she rolled to a halt. She had taken the record, covering 2,164 miles in 24 hours at an average speed of almost 90 m.p.h.

As she left the timekeeper's hut, she bumped into a friend from London, Earl Howe, who was racing the Bentley at Le Mans and who happened to be President of the British Racing Drivers' Club, the organisation that had grown out of informal dinners and gatherings at Benjafield's London home.

"I thought you'd do it", he said cheerily. "In fact I came down early from Paris this morning to watch your last few laps. Would you be too tired to drive with me to Paris and have some lunch?"[228] The Hon. Mrs Victor Bruce, tired? Not a bit of it, although she did admit to nodding off over coffee just as Earl Howe said he was going to propose that she be given honorary membership of the B.R.D.C.

CAPTAIN BIRKIN AND THE HON. DOROTHY PAGET.
To Captain Birkin for Lapping Up the Miles at 135.33 P.H., and to the Hon. Dorothy Paget for Going as His Mechanic in the Mountain Speed Handicap.

Captain Birkin beat Mr. Kaye Don's record at Brooklands by going at 135.33 m.p.h. The Hon. Dorothy Paget, who recently bought his team of racing cars, accompanied him in the Mountain Speed Handicap.

The other strong woman who barged her way into the de facto all-male-club known as the Bentley Boys was another aristocrat, the Hon. Dorothy Paget. In many ways she was the opposite of Mrs Bruce: although ten years younger than the petite, fashion-conscious record-breaker, she was at least ten stone heavier and took very little interest in her appearance.

It may be a cheap observation, but here was a woman who really was larger than life, and not what one might call conventionally attractive. One anecdote puts her appearance in context. In 1983 the Bentley Drivers Club unearthed a picture of Tim Birkin at the wheel of a Bentley discussing something with the Brooklands scrutineer; next to Tim in the car was, according to the caption given by the B.D.C., Woolf Barnato.[229] Except it wasn't. Closer examination of the picture revealed that it was not the chairman of Bentley Motors in drag but, rather, the Hon. Dorothy Paget.

The colossally rich and monumentally spoilt daughter of Lord Queenborough and the American heiress Pauline Whitney, Dorothy Wyndham Paget was an eccentric, who stood out even against the rich and colourful social backdrop of the 1920s. In her early teens, after trying out half a dozen of the better British boarding schools, she attended a school in Paris run by an exiled Russian princess, of whom she became very fond, and her sister Madame Orloff, the latter becoming her paid companion. While she was in Paris, it was discovered that she had a talent for singing, which she kept up on her return to London, giving a concert at Wormwood Scrubs.

Her aversion to men became noticeable in the early 1920s when, as a slim and attractive débutante, she came out and jilted every suitor who came her way. Her fortune was such that there was no shortage of potential husbands, and at the end of the 1924 season one Society wit suggested forming a club for those men who had been snubbed or otherwise turned down by this rich, wilful young woman. Her Sapphic tendencies were such that she allowed herself only one close male friend, a highly cultivated and extremely rich man called Sir Francis Cassel, who, as Paget's biographer Quintin Gilbey put it, 'was no more attracted to women than D.P. was to men'. In fact she once confided that the worst experience of her life took place in Paris when she was kissed by a man. Her reaction was allergic. "I rushed to the loo and threw up".[230]

By the time Dorothy was twenty years old, her father had given her a Rolls-Royce as a present and she had given up going to dances. She had also started playing cards and remained for the rest of her life an extremely heavy gambler, out of which was born her passion for the turf. She became a noted racehorse owner and was a conspicuous sight at race meetings – you could hardly miss her – wearing a lucky tweed overcoat that she called 'speckled hen' and a beret knitted by Madame Orloff.[231]

Impossibly rude (the older she got the more she hated meeting people and this was one way of keeping them at a distance), pathologically unpunctual (she would think nothing of keeping a member of her staff waiting for five hours) and a chain-smoker capable of getting through 100 Balkan Sobranies a day (smoked through a holder), she cared little for clothes, jewellery or visits to the hairdresser, instead indulging her appetite for food, which was reflected in her portly figure. On the face of it, she had little in common with the slight, dapper baronet's son and motor-racing ace Tim Birkin.

And yet, as the twenties turned into the thirties, these two great characters of the Jazz Age formed one of the most unlikely alliances of the day. Before she became hooked on horse racing, Dorothy Paget had become excited by motor racing. She put in an appearance at Brooklands and was thrilled by what she saw. Like

The Hon. Mrs Dorothy Paget riding alongside Sir Tim Birkin (opposite) at Brooklands where he set a speed record of 135.33 m.p.h.

The Welwyn Garden City workshops (below) where Birkin developed his Blower Bentleys under the patronage of Dorothy Paget.

THE GOLDEN YEARS

Birkin's Blower Bentleys in production on the factory floor and lined up outside the workshops.

everyone else in Britain, she was aware of the run of Bentley wins at Le Mans and, her disinclination towards the opposite sex notwithstanding, she could not have been ignorant of Tim Birkin, dare-devil Bentley Boy and (though the thought might have made her shudder) debonair lady's man. Dorothy was not exactly Tim's type, but she did have one thing that he was running rather short of: money.

Divorce, a hectic social life, frequent tailors' bills and a passion to see Britain taken seriously as a motor-racing nation had eaten up rather more of Tim's money than he liked to admit; it was at around this time that he moved out of Tacolneston Hall and rented nearby Shadwell Court. Towards the end of 1928 he had started looking for premises not too far from the Bentley works where he could establish a separate engineering works to develop what the Hon. Mrs Bruce might have called 'hotted-up' Bentleys. Early in 1929 he established such an operation in the newly built town of Welwyn Garden City just north of London. He was obsessed with getting more performance out of the 4½-litre Bentley by supercharging the engine. W.O. made no secret of his disapproval. 'To supercharge a Bentley engine was to pervert its design and corrupt its performance', he said rather bluntly in later life.[232] Nevertheless, Birkin prevailed upon Amherst Villiers to work on a supercharger and persuaded Barnato to agree to manufacture 50 such cars for sale, to enable the 'Blower Bentley' to qualify for Le Mans.[233]

Dorothy visited the Welwyn works in October 1929 and shortly after that became Tim's sponsor, throwing money at her stable of Bentleys much as she would later spend huge sums of money on horses. She took instruction from Tim and apparently became a very good driver, allegedly 'racing in public under a "Miss Wyndham" pseudonym'.[234] Birkin is said to have described her as 'one of the finest women drivers of fast cars he had ever come across, capable of handling any make of racing car produced in this country or abroad.'[235] Given the money she was pouring into his dream, it might have been ungallant for him to say otherwise; nevertheless, high-speed motoring in exotic

142

cars was to remain one of Dorothy Paget's traits for the rest of her life.

It is characteristic that Birkin viewed Dorothy Paget's gesture as more than the whim of a rich, eccentric young woman. Although the Bentley Boys undoubtedly enjoyed themselves hugely, some of them felt that there was a higher purpose to their endeavours, which imbued their exploits with a sense of epic grandeur. With Sammy, for instance, this was evident in the mythological allusions with which he peppered his writings, consciously or otherwise linking the racing drivers of the 1920s with the chivalric heroes of history and legend.

For Birkin, the higher purpose was patriotism; his motoring autobiography, *Full Throttle*, written in 1932, is memorable chiefly for its feeling of embittered national pride. As well as a colourful memoir of racing days, it is a splenetic polemic, inveighing against 'the present lethargy of the English motor industry' and what Birkin saw as a near-criminal indifference to Britain's standing in international motor sport.[236] In particular, he was appalled that Britain, during his time, never produced a Grand Prix car. Birkin raced his Bentley at Grands Prix, but it was not the same thing; he wanted Britain to boast 'a pure racing machine, built for that one purpose', the 'opposite to the Bentley and other English cars, which have competed in the races for standard models'.[237] The tenet of his argument was simple and is summed up in the following lines:

> It is not surprising that a nation's motor trade derives more impetus and publicity and financial profit from winning [Le Mans] than the most elaborate advertising campaign could ever give it. International prestige is of the greatest moment to the industry; and any country that does not exert its last breath to uphold its own, is guilty of unpardonable stupidity. We have committed that *crime* [my italics]; no real attempt has been made in England to *inculcate the all-importance* [my italics] of motor racing into the mind of the public, and when there is no public to arouse it, the idleness of manufacturers turns to stagnation. It is not so on the Continent; either the government has

CHAPTER SEVENTEEN

Dorothy was not exactly Tim's type, but she did have one thing he was running rather short of: money.

emphasised or the people themselves have been alive to the significance of their races; they have attended them unfailingly, and thereby aided them financially and guaranteed their continuity. But their enthusiasm has been appreciative, not merely excited by speed and the hope of accident. They know they are watching a spectacle, in which their country's reputation and part of its prosperity are at stake.[238]

Quite whether the average spectator at a continental Grand Prix of the 1920s was weighing up in his mind the macro-economic implications of every gear change and every corner taken is open to question, but Birkin's feelings are made admirably clear. He elaborates on his views at length, seeing the development of British motor racing as a panacea for many national ills. He fondly imagined that 'millions' would attend English races, that the excitement of the crowds would be 'leavened by intelligence in a desire to uphold the British motor market' and that the economy would benefit, with shopkeepers near races being 'able to retire after a few years' on the profits made from the crowds.

Nor does he omit the geo-political ramifications: the number of motor-racing enthusiasts flooding into Britain would bring with them 'the spirit of Kameradschaft or Fraternité' with the obvious result that 'international

> There was gossip that Birkin did more than instruct this young woman in the mysteries of the motor.

relations would be aided by a voluntary friendship far stronger than political entente'.[239] He juxtaposes this vision of an utopia based on motor racing with what he saw as the pathetic reality: he does not hold back, even taking a swipe at Brooklands, a site of near-religious significance to the British motoring enthusiast, which he described as being 'without exception, the most out-of-date, inadequate and dangerous track in the world'.[240] Ouch!

The fact that these views were expressed by a slightly built, stuttering, dandified ladies' man, a blasé playboy who lived for the thrills of motor racing, meant that they were easy to dismiss. However, at the time of writing this book, not one major British automotive marque remains in British hands. Many of the names with which Birkin would have been familiar have ceased to exist, others, including Bentley and Rolls-Royce, have been bought by overseas investors who now make rather better cars than was the case when the marques were in British ownership.

Birkin was clearly obsessed. Having dissipated much of his fortune in pursuit of automotive glory, having sensed that with the slide of the New York stock market the world economy would suffer and, despairing of any support from either British industry or the state, he clung to Dorothy Paget as to a life raft. In 1930 he wrote:

> At the beginning of the new year, it was announced that a fairy godmother in the earthly guise of the Hon. Dorothy Paget, had come to the Cinderella of British motor industry. She bought in March my three Bentleys, among them the track single-seater which was begun at the end of 1929, and increased them to four. Hers was a most sporting action, prompted by a genuine sympathy with a cause in which she herself was well-versed; it gave a new lease of life to the motor-racing world in England, and indeed it seems to be women who have, and use generously, the disposal of that lease. The cars were, of course, her property, but I was to run them for her under the famous green colours.[241]

Inevitably, there was gossip that Birkin did more than instruct this young woman in the mysteries of the motor: there is speculation that there was a romantic dimension to the Birkin-Paget partnership, however unlikely, or indeed comical, that may sound. Decades later, her obituary in *Sporting Life* hinted very broadly that Dorothy had developed a fondness for the snappily dressed little racing driver, saying that when she pulled out of Birkin's Bentley team in 1931, she was, 'so it was rumoured, not entirely heart-whole'.[242]

Certainly, she seemed to have conquered her aversion to men to a sufficient degree to have been able to sit next to Birkin in the cockpit of a racing Bentley. She was a passenger when he lapped Dublin's Phoenix Park at 80 m.p.h. and, when she got out, said "I must do a lot more of it."[243] If, indeed, Birkin had succeeded in seducing this young woman and making her fall in love with him, it would have been an achievement at least equal to his heroic and theatrical performances on the racetrack. If he considered it at all, he presumably thought that one young woman's heart was worth breaking in his pursuit of glory.

Paget's Bentley Blowers in action at Brooklands, on the banking at high speed (opposite, above) and Tim Birkin in 1930 being push started (opposite, below).

CHAPTER EIGHTEEN

even though the

New York stock market collapse at the end of the preceding year had destroyed many fortunes, the French Riviera was still thronged with royalty, aristocracy and plutocracy during the early spring of 1930. During February and March, the fashionable resort of Cannes filled up with its usual habitués: the Marquess and Marchioness of Huntly came to visit the Prince and Princess of Hesse, who were at the Villa Mariposa, while Anne Countess of Mexborough was to be found a little further down the coast at Juan-les-Pins.

That year, the Hôtel des Anglais was favoured by blue bloods from Russia and Greece, including Grand Duchess Helène of Russia, and Princesses Nicholas, Elisabeth and Marina of Greece.[244] The English, meanwhile, bestowed their patronage on the Carlton, which, with its extravagant décor, was a true throwback to the opulence of the Belle Epoque. The Carlton Hotel had opened before the First World War; a great white palace, it dominated the Croisette and had spectacular views out over the Mediterranean. Its twin cupolas were reputedly modelled on the breasts of the era's favourite femme fatale, La Belle Otero, whose lovers included Edward VII, the King of Spain, the Tsar of Russia, Reza Shah and the King of Belgium, as well as assorted millionaires. Among those staying at the Carlton that year were Viscount and Viscountess Scarsdale, Sir James and Lady Carmichael, Sir Percy Simmons and that fashionable young man, chairman of Bentley Motors, Captain Woolf Barnato.[245]

Barnato loved the Riviera. Its mixture of sportiness and hedonism suited him perfectly and he enjoyed the invigorating drive down, especially when he had someone like Rubin around who also had the time and money on his hands to make the drive more competitive. Kidston, too, was often down on the Côte d'Azur, as were many other Bentley owners.

Given his fondness for having his photograph taken, Barnato must have loved the attention the Society pages bestowed upon him there, and one year, after, as was usual, his name had been mentioned in the press roll-call of visitors to the South of France, he threw a steak-and-kidney-pie party, to which all Bentley owners on the coast were invited. During dinner, Barnato announced that he had placed a Bentley mechanic at a local garage, ready to carry out adjustments – free of charge, naturally. This man was on hand to deal with, among other things, a faulty starter motor for the King of Sweden and repairs to the Bentley belonging to 'a titled couple', who turned up 'tight as owls' very 'early one morning, straight from an all-night pyjama party'.[246]

However, in the spring of 1930 there was one recurring topic of conversation among the British visitors as they settled into their lavish suites at the Carlton: the new motoring fashion of racing the Blue Train.

With the exception of the Orient Express, the Blue Train, or 'le Train Bleu', is one of the most evocative railway trains ever to take to the tracks. So-called because it was painted blue at a time when most rolling stock was a boring brown, its quotidian, official name was the Calais-Méditerranée-Express'.

Like Bentley Motors, the Blue Train made its début at the beginning of the Roaring Twenties, on 8 December 1922. The South of France was still considered primarily a winter destination, only gaining popularity as a summer playground for the international set as the 1920s wore on. It was not until 1923 that Coco Chanel made summer on the Riviera fashionable, when she sashayed down the gangplank of the Duke of Westminster's yacht, tanned a daring shade of nut brown; hitherto a suntan had marked its wearer as an agricultural labourer. In Mary Blume's book *Côte d'Azur, Inventing the French Riviera*, Prince Jean-Louis de Faucigny-Lucinge is quoted as

Barnato loved the Riviera. Its mixture of sportiness and hedonism suited him perfectly.

Barnato at Cannes in 1931 (previous page), with a Miss P. Matthews, leaning against his Le Mans winning car having recently retired from racing.

saying, "I think she may have invented sunbathing, at that time she invented everything".

In those days of prelapsarian innocence before melanoma was linked to soaking up the sun's rays, European high society would board the Blue Train in search of the sun. It was, in effect, a gateway to decadence and became as much a symbol of the era as the cars emblazoned with the winged 'B'. During the 1920s this train was shamelessly sybaritic. Its sole purpose was to transport the carefree rich to their villas and hotel suites in the South of France as quickly as possible. To make the journey more bearable, there were luxury sleeping and dining carriages capable of accommodating 80 people in what, for those who led more humdrum lives, was unimaginable comfort.

However, as the twenties ended, so, too, did the hegemony of this evocative rail service. During the early months of 1930 first a Rover, then an Alvis raced the Blue Train from the Côte d'Azur to Calais and won. The Rover finished ahead of the train by 20 minutes; the Alvis managed to complete the journey three hours earlier than the rail passengers.

It would have been unnatural for Barnato, a proud and competitive man, not to have been at least slightly piqued that rival car-makers had pulled off a valuable publicity coup at a time when sales of any marque would have benefited from a boost. And when one of them placed advertisements bragging about the feat, Barnato's pique turned to irritation. After all, Bentley, not Rover, not Alvis, was the premier sporting marque in Britain. And besides, the way Barnato saw it, beating the Blue Train from the Mediterranean coast to the English Channel with a modern car was not the great achievement that it might have seemed. When the train had started its service, it had been swift and reliable, but that was eight years earlier, and automotive design had come an awfully long way since then.

If his friends at the bar of the Carlton Hotel ribbed him about the record-breaking achievements of Rover and Alvis, Barnato retorted that "the achievements advertised did not deserve much merit".[247] And just in case anyone thought it was sour grapes, Barnato offered a wager that he could get to England in his Speed Six Saloon before the train reached Calais.

Those who had been teasing Barnato would have fallen silent for a moment. It was known that Babe was not the sort of man to offer a wager unless he was pretty sure that he would win. Once he embarked on an endeavour, little could divert him until he achieved his goal. At first his cronies tried to laugh it off as a bit of late-night bravado; but Barnato was serious. When it became clear that this was not the idle cocktail-fuelled boast of a dilettante playboy, there were no takers for the wager. Obviously the drinks had not been flowing quite long enough for anyone to take up Barnato's bet.

But the prospect of winning or losing money on the outcome no longer really mattered. Barnato had set himself a challenge and, while he genuinely discounted the achievement of Rover and Alvis, he could not let such a pair of rather ordinary British automotive marques have the glory of beating the evocative Blue Train.

"All right", he said, after a moment's reflection, "we'll have 'no bet', but I say I shall do it, just to prove my contention that beating the Blue Train deserves little merit." And, with the gauntlet thrown down, Barnato prepared for what he called an "unofficial run" with all the meticulous care and minute planning that characterised the marque's spectacular victories at La Sarthe.[248]

Evidently he had already given the challenge some thought before he made his apparently spontaneous remark that beating the Blue Train was no 'great shakes'. He had, quite intentionally, not stipulated that he would follow the route taken by the Blue Train, but merely that he would leave Cannes at the same time as the Blue Train and arrive in England before the train had pulled into Calais. In this he was rather cunning, having researched the railway timetable and noted that from Cannes the train chugged along the coast to Marseilles, where it stopped for an hour before heading up to Paris, where it took a further three and a half hours getting across town, before continuing to the Channel.

As the train travelled west to Marseilles, Barnato planned to leave Cannes, striking out north to make for Boulogne. A fairer test might have been to race the

Blue Train from Marseilles: the chances are he would have won … but not by the convincing margin that he needed to show that the 'achievement' of beating the Blue Train was in fact no such thing.

He arranged petrol supplies at four-hourly intervals along his route and, just in case, he filled his boot with cans of petrol. Indeed, such was the quantity of extra fuel he loaded that the tail weight of his car precluded him travelling at more than 80 m.p.h. without causing damage to the springs. However, he calculated that prolonged high-speed driving would have been unnecessary to beat the Blue Train and anyway, driving at night on French country roads in 1930 there would have been little opportunity for the flat-out motoring of which the Speed Six was capable. Barnato chose Dale Bourne, a famous amateur golfer who was also on the Riviera, as co-driver, in the event that he should tire at the wheel.

On the afternoon of Thursday 13 March, having left nothing to chance, Barnato and his passenger went for a drink. He later recalled:

> We waited in the Carlton Bar till we got word from the station that the train had left (5.54pm), we finished our drinks and left. At Aix-en-Provence we topped up with petrol (100 miles). Knowing how difficult it is to get 'gas' at night in France, I had already arranged for a garage pump I knew at Lyons to remain open till after midnight, and for a petrol lorry to be at Auxerre at 4 a.m. I arrived at the pump in Lyons at one minute to midnight (nicely up to schedule). From Lyons onwards it poured with rain which put us a bit behind schedule, so that we didn't get to Auxerre till 4.20 a.m., and then had difficulty in locating the petrol lorry which had gone into town instead of staying on the by-pass. After Auxerre, on the high ground, we ran into the cloud front that had been dealing out the rain. The result of which was we were three-quarters of an hour behind schedule getting to Paris. Soon after leaving Paris I burst a tyre and as I only had one spare wheel I had to take it easy as another blow-out would have meant I'd 'had-it'. Happy to relate, no other untoward incident took place from there onwards, and I pulled on to the Quai at Boulogne at 10.30 a.m.
>
> The Boulogne-Folkestone boat used to leave at 11.30 so that it gave the R.A.C. the requisite hour they require for a car to be at the port before sailing, and ourselves good time to have an excellent breakfast in the station buffet. In fact, my car was the first on and, therefore, the first off at Folkestone.
>
> A pleasant one hour twenty minutes' sea trip, no trouble at the Customs, and super-efficient service by the R.A.C. on the triptyque business (word seemed to have preceded us that we were to be given priority), and we were again away before the train left Folkestone for London. We cruised slowly to London Town, for after all, the mission of getting to England first had already been completed, and we saw no reason to hurry, especially in view of the fact that I now had no spare wheel.
>
> On getting to London I noticed the clock at Victoria on the Vauxhall Bridge road signified the time as 3.20 p.m. I said to Dale, "Do you know we've got to London before the train has got to Calais." (The train reaches Calais at 3.24 p.m.) So to confirm this we clocked in at Bourne's Club, the Conservative in St. James' Street. Then I thought we ought to register our arrival with the R.A.C. The news of our successful run had apparently already preceded us, for the hall porter was waiting with the time clock message stamping machine to "mark our cards."[249]

Barnato was recalling the event a couple of years before his death, and yet that all-night drive was still very fresh in his mind, as was the sportsman's excitement at a challenge. But there is perhaps a slightly disingenuous tone to the whole thing. The quick passage through customs, the helpful R.A.C., the chance glance at the clock at Victoria Station … Barnato's elaborate insouciance seems to belie a mounting sense of triumph at making it not just to England, but to London clubland, before the Blue Train pulled into Calais.

This episode makes it very clear how much his association with Bentley meant to Barnato. It gave him réclame and a position in Society that no amount of money could have bought. At that exultant moment at the hall porter's desk Barnato entered the pantheon of British 'have-a-go heroes'.

The Blue Train run became a potent part of the Bentley legend, in a way far more characteristic of the marque than its records at Le Mans. It mixed the high life of Cannes, the stamina-sapping, long-distance drive in varying weather conditions, the outstanding reliability of a Bentley, the drama of a blown tyre, the hushed world of the London club and the nationalistic gratification of beating the French.

Ironically, as the years passed, the Blue Train run became a legend in a way that Barnato could never have foreseen. Far from showing how inconsequential beating the Blue Train was, this episode is enshrined in Bentley lore. Today no one talks of the '"Blue Train" Alvis' or '"Blue Train" Rover', but, despite it having been proved that it was another car entirely[250], Barnato's rakishly bodied Gurney Nutting coupé has inspired owners to build replica 'Blue Train' Bentleys. And the 'race' has been celebrated in totally fanciful artists' impressions of the wrong car racing alongside the fabled express, even though, as Barnato's account makes clear, he took an entirely different route. Looking back, it was also something of a swan song for the carefree *carpe diem* attitude of the Roaring Twenties – the Thirties would unfold to the tramp of jackboots rather than the roar of big displacement engines. At the time, however, it was just another one of those japes that were a natural consequence of an excess of money, fun and horsepower.

In order to stop the British motorist using the roads of France for impromptu speed trials, and perhaps to salve the wounded pride of le Train Bleu, the French authorities came down rather hard on Barnato, and Bentley was barred from the Paris Motor Salon. They took the attitude that as chairman of Bentley Motors, Barnato had undertaken the run on a professional level to promote the marque.

His response was the slightly disingenuous one that he was nothing more than a private citizen having a bit of a lark, albeit a lark with a co-driver, pre-arranged fuel stops and boot full of petrol acting as a *de facto* reserve tank.

> At that exultant moment at the hall porter's desk Barnato entered the pantheon of British 'have-a-go heroes'.

It was unfortunate that Bentleys were barred from the Paris Salon of 1930 for this escapade, on the grounds that we'd advertised an unofficial trial, although we put no advertisement in at all; naturally the Press got hold of the story and wrote it up. As I was the then chairman of Bentleys, this was considered advertising, when in reality the whole thing was done to show that there was no great merit in beating the Blue Train.[251]

His daughter Diana Barnato Walker remembers that he "always said it wasn't a bet, merely a wager between friends".[252]

Despite the publicity generated, the absence of Bentley from the Paris Salon probably did the company no harm; by 1930 it was clear that the world economy was in no position to support the luxury car market. Moreover, it was also gradually becoming apparent that Barnato was increasing less inclined to keep the financially insecure company afloat. However, while it might not be making an appearance at the Paris Motor Salon, Bentley would certainly be represented at Le Mans.

Chapter Nineteen

Rudolf Carraciola

His parents had wanted him to go into the family hotel business, but at the age of fourteen he decided that he wanted to be a motor-racing driver. 'I believe that every man can achieve the goal he strives for' was his maxim.[253] In 1926 he had won the German Grand Prix at the wheel of a Mercedes. He was just 22. His style was somewhat different from the romantic notions in which the British drivers wrapped their racing:

was a machine.

To be a racing driver means to have the ability to be for hours on end a part of the machine – hand on wheel and on gearshift, feet on throttle and brake, eyes on the speedometer, the water and oil thermometer. Woe to him who, even for the fraction of a second, loses control over himself! One never allows extraneous emotions or thoughts to arise in the crucial hour of the race. The machine will crush him mercilessly. Woe to those who relinquish control over themselves to a passion, be it the passion for women, for drink or for any other addiction. They become unsure of themselves, they lose, along with self-control, mastery of the machine, and their fate is to be eliminated or to die.[254]

As the 1920s drew to a close, title after title fell to his iron nerve, his high speeds and unerring judgement. At the wheel of his Mercedes, he swept all competition before him without a flicker of fear or emotion. He would sleep until an hour or two before the start of a race, arriving shortly before the flag fell, step into his giant, white, 7-litre, supercharged Mercedes and drive more or less flat out, achieving top speeds of 125 m.p.h. 'I can recall no time at which he has been guilty of recklessness or inaccuracy', wrote one of his greatest admirers, and rivals, Tim Birkin.[255]

Although an unqualified admirer of Carraciola, Birkin was his opposite; older, excitable, a risk-taker and a romantic with a touch of melancholy, he could only marvel in slack-jawed amazement at the performance of Carraciola and his Mercedes. The Mercedes was faster and more powerful than the Bentley, so Birkin, of course, wanted to beat it.

Bentley and Mercedes dominated the 1920s, but with supercharged cars and a star driver, Mercedes appeared to be getting the upper hand towards the end of the decade. Of the 1928 race at the Nürburgring circuit, Birkin wrote frustratedly, 'We were hopelessly outclassed in the unsupercharged Bentleys by the giant supercharged Mercs.' In that race, Birkin finished eighth, and it was little comfort that the chairman of Mercedes congratulated him on his car's performance, saying that "its running was so accurate, and its lapping so regular, that people almost set their watches by it".[256] As Birkin said, 'to the German mind such precision had a particular appeal'. W.O., too, valued the reliable performance of an unstressed engine above all else. Birkin and his large fairy godmother, however, were concentrating on creating a supercharged British car.

While Birkin had been busy, Carraciola and the Mercedes team had not been idle either. In 1929 the 7-litre Mercedes with Carraciola at the wheel had won in torrential rain at the Ards circuit in Northern Ireland, pushing Birkin into a humiliating eleventh place. Rather more alarmingly, the Mercedes team had studied the Bentley team's winning Le Mans

Caracciola's works Mercedes SSK at the 1930 Le Mans (previous page).

Man or machine? The Mercedes driver Rudolf Caracciola (above and opposite, top) drove with an awesome, almost inhuman precision. In 1930 he was pitted against the romantic melancholic British baronette and Bentley Boy Sir Henry 'Tim' Birkin (opposite, below).

> There is little doubt that all five Bentleys intended to work together to bring down the lone giant white sports car on which German hopes and British fears rested.

strategy and lap times and had set about devising a plan to snatch victory there for themselves in 1930. It hardly needs to be said that Bentley regarded Le Mans, more than any other contest, as its own property.

By 1930 the shockwaves of the Wall Street Crash were washing through Europe: sales of sports and luxury cars were suffering, cutbacks were being made; the decade-long party of the 1920s was all but over. There were only eighteen starters at Le Mans that year, but of the cars lining up on the afternoon of 21 June, five were Bentleys: three factory prepared cars and two of Birkin's 'Blowers'.

No doubt sensing the power of the Mercedes challenge and the German marque's remarkable young driver, W.O. had entered into a Faustian pact with the supercharger, a device he regarded as the devil's work. It has become part of Bentley lore that W.O. was opposed to the Blower, his opinion famously being that the supercharged 4½-litre 'brought the *marque* Bentley disrepute'.[257] However, it is possible to detect a whiff of revisionism in W.O.'s tendency in later life to blame the Blower for hastening the demise of an independent Bentley Motors.

Indeed, Benjafield ascribes the idea of a supercharged Bentley to W.O. himself, saying that W.O. mentioned supercharging the 3-litre in November 1924 as a way of getting more power, although nothing was done.[258] Moreover, when he talks of the work undertaken on the Blower, Benjafield includes W.O. in the list of those who were involved:

> During the autumn and early winter of 1929, Tim Birkin, assisted by many others, notably H. Kensington Moir, Bernard Rubin, Beris Harcourt Wood, Clive Gallop, and Captain W.O. Bentley on the technical side, put into practice a scheme which had been incubating in the minds of most of us for some considerable time, viz., to supercharge the 4½.[259]

W.O.'s involvement with the supercharger project was apparent at the Belfast T.T. of August 1929 (a race in which Kidston crashed and Rubin rolled his car), when Birkin entered three supercharged Bentleys, one of which he drove himself with W.O. riding with him as race mechanic. The winner of the race was, of course, Carraciola.

Benjy's is a very different view to W.O.'s: while the former saw the Blower as a project supported by many, including W.O. himself, the latter tended to present it as an obsession of Birkin's, made possible through investment by Dorothy Paget and Birkin's persuasiveness in getting Barnato to build 50 Blowers to homologate the model for Le Mans. Although W.O. made it known that he regarded Birkin's team as a competitor — the two teams even wore different ties (red and grey for drivers of the Blowers, the colours in which Tim had his non-racing Bentleys; green stripes on a dark blue background for drivers of normally aspirated cars, designed by Sammy Davis[260])[261] — there is little doubt that all five Bentleys intended to

work together to bring down the lone giant white sports car on which German hopes and British fears rested.

Sammy Davis recalls the pre-race wrangling:

> Tim was very fast, very fast indeed, but it was not easy to suggest to him that his car's chance of finishing was not too great, so that his natural tactical rôle was to go flat out and try and push the Mercedes; it was all very difficult, because Tim, by nature exactly suited for this task, wanted especially to finish.
>
> Lengthy discussions went on until, finally, Tim agreed to the suggestion, his car being backed up by my six-cylinder, with Barnato's, then Clement's in support, while the other supercharged cars [in fact only one other supercharged car entered] were to drive to finish.[262]

It was a particularly important race for the Bentley Boys: for Barnato there was the tantalising prospect of a hat-trick, for Bentley Motors there was the chance of a fourth win in a row, while Birkin wanted to prove the value of his supercharged car in the eyes of the world (and W.O.). But before any of these things could happen, the threat posed by the Mercedes of Carraciola had to be dealt with.

But before the flag dropped on that momentous Le Mans there was an afternoon of rapprochement between the three-pointed star and the winged 'B'. The tension that year between the two teams must have been unbearable. Perhaps in order to tone things down, the Automobile Club de l'Ouest held a lunch for the Bentley and Mercedes teams. It 'took place in

Birkin's 4½ Litre Blowers powered along the Mulsanne Straight during the 1930 Le Mans, reaching speeds of up to 125m.p.h.

a beautiful old hotel, a river running at the end of its pleasant garden, on one of the finest days imaginable'.[263] At first the mood was tense, but when Moritz, a dog presumably belonging to the Mercedes team, fell into the river and had to be rescued, the atmosphere lightened. And as more wine was consumed, the language barriers were broken down and, as Sammy recalled, 'the lunch party was an immense success, we all ended up with toasts in the English, French, and German manner, so that we did not break up until nearly dinner time'.[264] However, Sammy kept his ears open and it was apparently at this lunch that one of the Mercedes team let slip that his side was very happy with the performance of the car, provided the supercharger was not used too much. This vital piece of information determined Bentley's race strategy.

At 4p.m. on Saturday 21 June, on a dusty ten-mile track in the middle of France, the last and greatest automotive duel of a truly golden and chivalric era of motor sport began. The Mercedes got off to a good start, but almost immediately Birkin put the pressure on and passed it, losing the tread of his tyre in the process. He continued to drive on until the tyre burst and he limped into the pits for a wheel change, allowing Carraciola to slacken off the supercharger.

A couple of hours later, Clive Dunfee put one of the Speed Sixes into a sandbank and, although he and Sammy Davis (who had splinters of glass in his eye) dug it out, the car was undriveable.

By the early evening, with the Blowers having persistent tyre trouble, Carraciola was ahead. However, through consistently excellent driving, Barnato kept in touch with the Mercedes and forced Carraciola to use the supercharger to retain his lead. During the night Bentley and Mercedes jockeyed for the lead, Barnato slowly building up speed on every lap, until at last, on the 83rd lap, the Mercedes went into the pits and did not emerge again, the team citing dynamo failure.[265] After that the Bentley drastically reduced its speed, adhering to W.O.'s rule that a car should never go faster than absolutely necessary to win a race. The Blowers

> At 4p.m. on Saturday 21 June, on a dusty ten-mile track in the middle of France, the last and greatest automotive duel of a truly golden and chivalric era of motor sport began.

Clement and Watney's Bentley leads Benjafield and Ramponi's car at the 1930 Le Mans (opposite). Clement and Watney finished in 2nd position.

Ditched in a sandbank, Clive Dunfee put the car he was driving with Sammy Davis out of the 1930 Le Mans race at the notorious Pontlieue bend.

THE GOLDEN YEARS

The Bentley crew get to work on the Speed Six of Clement and Watney during an evening pitstop during the 24 hour race of the 1930 Le Mans.

Barnato and Kidston's Speed Six, No. 4 (above), took 1st position at the 1930 Le Mans race.

Wearing the victor's laurels, Kidston and Barnato celebrate their win (opposite) flanked by Clement and Watney, who took 2nd place also in a Bentley Speed Six.

THE GOLDEN YEARS

Kidston steers the winning Bentley on a victory lap (above), with Barnato as his passenger, following their 1930 Le Mans win.

A contemporary newspaper report of the announcement of Barnato's decision to withdraw Bentley from motor racing (opposite, above).

Relaxing at Cannes, his retirement from motor racing left Barnato free to follow other leisure pursuits (opposite, below).

eventually dropped out, Birkin at noon, with valve trouble, Benjy an hour later with a broken piston. It was Kidston who crossed the finishing line in first place, sharing the victor's laurels with Barnato.

A great drama played out to the soundtrack of the thunder of the Bentley and the banshee-like wail of the Mercedes supercharger, the 1930 Le Mans has become a part of the Bentley legend almost as mighty as the White House Crash.

The press reception was rapturous. Typically effusive was the *Daily Express* of 23 June: under the banner headline 'Drama of New British Speed Victory', and a further headline 'Millionaire wins for England', the story was recounted with heightened drama. For his gallantry, Tim Birkin's portrait photograph was reproduced, while Barnato had to make do with a less distinct picture of himself at the wheel.

The Mercedes was vanquished, Barnato got his hat-trick and the firm got its fourth consecutive win at Le Mans. As the works driver, Clement's impressive record mirrored that of Bentley. As Darell Berthon points out in *A Racing History of the Bentley*, 'It is worth mentioning here that Frank Clement is the only driver to have competed in the same make of car, 3-, 4½- and 6½-litre, for eight consecutive races at Le Mans, i.e. from the first event in 1923 until 1930.'[266]

Shortly after that glorious Le Mans, Bentley announced its withdrawal from motor racing. The worsening business climate did not favour luxury marques such as Bentley. Moreover, having won so publicly and so frequently at Le Mans, all that Bentley risked now was tarnishing the lustre of its victories. 'Our retirement from racing after Le Mans was strongly criticized at the time', said W.O., 'but I'm sure it was the right thing to do'.[267] Probably it was the only thing to do. Michael Hay pithily sums up the position of Bentley motors at its moment of triumph at Le Mans: 'The Company was effectively bust by June 1930.'[268]

Bust or not, there was going to be a celebration, and this time Ardenrun was the venue for a 'farewell-to-motor-racing' party. By August, Kidston, Barnato *et al* were on the Riviera, Kidston having flown himself down in a small Puss Moth aeroplane. A photograph in the *Sketch* shows Babe in a 'natty beach suit, worn with an American sailor's cap'.[269] In the evenings the party would put on more formal clothes and move to the casinos where, while the world moved ever deeper into the Great Depression, tens of thousands of pounds changed hand over cards. One member of Kidston's party, Jack Coats, lost £80,000 in an evening, which put Barnato's losses at Bentley into some sort of perspective.[270]

Besides, there was plenty to take his mind off the financial problems of Bentley Motors, as the following item in the *Evening Standard* shows:

> 'Cocktail' racing is a highly popular amusement at Cannes. Some six or seven luxury speed-boats, driven by such well-known people as Mr. 'Babe' Barnato (whose 'drinking' partner, as the other member of the crew was known, was Captain 'Babe' White, one of the biggest people ever seen on the plage), Captain Glen Kidston, the well-known racing motorist, Major Jack Coats, the millionaire, in his great Bon partout, which cost £21,000, and Mrs Louis Beaumont, one of the best-dressed women in the South, and the wife of Commodore Beaumont, competed in one race. Mr. Farman, in his Mona, won after a contest lasting nearly an hour.
>
> Both driving and 'drinking' members of the team had to consume quite a number of cocktails, and the way in which they handled the launches and swam to the rafts to be picked up at the various calling points in the race was greatly admired.
>
> The landing steps had to be continually cleared in order to allow the dripping competitors to rush up to the cocktail tables and seize their cocktails, before diving in again for their next swim to the waiting launches.[271]

November saw Barnato shooting at Shadwell with Prince George and Tim Birkin, and the following month he was in America with Glen Kidston, where the two men bet £150 over the provenance of a bottle of bootleg whisky. Late winter/early spring 1931 saw him skiing in Switzerland. Barnato did not seem to be having too much difficulty in moving on from the Bentley era.

Chapter Twenty

For others, the news of Bentley's withdrawal from motor sport came as a terrible shock.

Benjafield recalled it thus:

As we said good-bye the following morning to all our good friends, little did any of us think that 1930 was the last time Bentley Motors Ltd., would compete at Le Mans. Of course we knew that the Company had weathered several financial crises in the past, but never in our blackest moods had we ever considered the possibility of the complete eclipse of the company that had produced these wonderful cars, for the sake of a few thousand pounds. Surely such a car was a national asset, an asset sufficiently valuable to be subsidized by the state rather than that it should be permitted to be swamped by some jiggery-pokery. This Bentley Motor-car was not just a plaything for the wealthy, a toy for 'The Bentley Boys'. A term manufactured by the press. I, for one, was proud to be associated with the Bentley Team, but we did not altogether appreciate being described as 'The Bentley Boys'.[272]

Kidston competing in the Irish International Grand Prix, at Phoenix Park, Dublin, passing George Eyston's Bugatti being extinguished after a stream of flames was seen shooting from under the car and from the petrol tank. Kidston lost to Boris Ivanovsky's Alfa Romeo by just 14 seconds.

But the problem was just that: the Bentley was perceived as a toy for rich playboys. In the years following the First World War, rich men in fast cars had been an amusing diversion, an agreeable antidote to the horrors of Passchendaele and the Somme. But the Bentley Boys had passed their sell-by date: everything, even motor-sport, was about to get much more serious. The world was entering what one historian called the 'Dark Valley' of the 1930s.[273] In the decade of the Spanish Civil War, the Great Depression, the rise of Nazism and the purges and show trials of Stalin's U.S.S.R., there would be little place for the Champagne-fuelled antics of Barnato and co.

Although the drivers may have personally disliked the term 'Bentley Boys', it cannot be denied that it had been good for the marque. The newsworthy nature of Bentley's rich, dashing customers had greatly assisted in keeping the company afloat for so long. Much has been made of W.O.'s expertise as an engineer, but he was also a shrewd judge of character, a manipulator of men and a marketing genius. He knew that the glamour of the Bentley Boys would keep *his* automotive marque alive. (Barnato may have owned the company, but in many ways W.O. remained the boss, and even Barnato deferred to him on the racetrack.)

If he had an eye to posterity, W.O. would have seen that the Bentley Boys would perpetuate the spirit of the marque. It can be argued that while W.O. built the cars, the Bentley Boys built the brand: without their seductive air of irresponsible thrill-seeking, Bentley would have amounted to nothing more than an interesting footnote in automotive history – an under-funded British sports-car marque that enjoyed competitive success but was snuffed out by the worldwide recession of the 1930s. Instead, the Bentley became a status symbol: in the novels of Ian Fleming, James Bond was a devotee of the marque; for rich parvenus a vintage Bentley lent a patina of age to their money; and when Bentleys and Rolls-Royces were made together, it was the Bentley that was seen as the more gentlemanly choice.

When the fortunes of the Bentley marque revived at the end of the twentieth century with the arrival of two-ton, turbo-charged cars capable of accelerating to 60 m.p.h. in under six seconds, it was the sporting era of Le Mans, Birkin, Barnato *et al* that was invoked with names including Mulsanne, Brooklands and Arnage. And when Team Bentley finished third at Le Mans in 2001, the team of drivers, inevitably dubbed the Bentley Boys, mounted the podium in twenties-style overalls; the cheers of

> Without their seductive air of irresponsible thrill-seeking, Bentley would have amounted to nothing.

approval left no doubt that the allusion to the days of the original Bentley Boys had been appreciated.

To use a term that was not current back in the 1920s and 1930s, the Bentley Boys were not politically correct. Nevertheless it is a mistake to view them as nothing more than two-dimensional, skirt-chasing playboys with more money than sense. They enjoyed life, but they were larger than life. They defined their times.

Their values are best expressed by some private letters of Kidston's, now in the possession of his nephew. These were not intended for publication and as such are unlike either the impassioned, polemical writings of the frustrated Tim Birkin or the revisionist memoirs of W.O. In August of 1930 Kidston was enjoying himself on the Côte d'Azur, but he found the time to write a twenty-page letter to his younger brother. In it, he offers plenty of fraternal advice. Typical of the sentiments expressed is this paragraph:

> Don't worry too much about what other people think about you – just go your own way, and don't be put off by following the mediocre examples of others! I struck out pretty much on my own, and never regretted it. If you follow the crowd you get nowhere – except the slough of despond. If you just want a good time and nothing else my few words of advice are worthless! But I do not feel you want to lead this kind of aimless existence! Life is not merely a procession of amusements – it is a serious business, and we, those better placed and better educated than our compatriots have a duty firstly to our country & secondly to the world, of showing some return for our mortal span on mother earth! We may be one of several tens of millions, but that does not relieve ourselves from making an effort.[274]

The fact that these noble sentiments are expressed on notepaper from the Majestic Hotel in Cannes neatly encapsulates the sybaritic and serious sides of the life of a Bentley Boy.

In another intimate letter, a love letter in fact, certainly never intended to be read by more than one pair of eyes, Kidston expresses similar sentiments, saying that he did not think that the object of his affection 'would care for me the least little bit if I just spent my life gadding around the dear old Embassy and places like that'. He continues thus:

> I've been bitten for years with an awful complex of ambition. Often I wished to God I had not had any ambition. It is a most disturbing instinct, yet I feel one is not made just to exist. Life, I imagine, is given to man or woman – more particularly man – to do something with. Mere existence to me is just wasting one's life.
>
> Because one has means is, to my way of thinking, a greater reason why one should strive to do something. The fellow who has to earn his own living has an excuse for doing nothing.

> They enjoyed life, but they were larger than life. They defined their times.

W.O. in later life, with models of the cars that bore his name.

At heart I am a bit of a socialist. Not that I despise money or that I do not appreciate its value – God forbid! But I feel one should try to do something and do it to the best of one's ability.[275]

It is a fair assumption to say that for all of the Bentley Boys the 1920s were the happiest days of their lives … even if they did not know it at the time.

By the end of 1930 W.O. was no longer Managing Director of Bentley Motors, although he continued as head of engineering. After Le Mans Bentley launched two models: the 8-litre – a fabulous car that was in many ways W.O.'s dream, a car capable of travelling at 100 m.p.h. in near silence – and the execrable 4-litre – a cheap, underpowered car cobbled together using the same chassis as the 8-litre to try and undercut the small Rolls-Royce. The 8-litre was too expensive for its time; the 4-litre was a half-hearted attempt from which W.O., understandably resentful at his removal as M.D., took care to distance himself in later years.

By the end of 1931 Bentley had been sold to its rival Rolls-Royce and W.O. was kept on in the humiliating position of a glorified test driver. After he left Rolls-Royce, W.O. worked at Lagonda, with which he returned to Le Mans one more time in 1939. After the Second World War he settled down to rural retirement in the Home Counties while the cult of the Bentley marque grew around him. He died in 1971.

Woolf Barnato with his second wife Jackie, on board the *Empress of Britain* in 1932.

M. Marioni (Alfa Romeo) passing the wreck of Glen Kidston's Bentley on Bradshaw's Brae.

THE GOLDEN YEARS

> Glen Kidston had seemed indestructible, having been torpedoed in the war and survived the break up of his powerboat at speed.

Woolf Barnato merely lost money. "I know nearly a hundred thousand went down the drain in Bentley Motors", he is reported to have said, "but on one diamond deal during that time I made a hundred and twenty thousand, so I can't grumble".[276] He won a seat on the board of Bentley Motors (1931) Ltd., as the company became known under the ownership of Rolls-Royce. He married for the second time, but continued to maintain a dilatory interest in motor racing, building Bentley specials with Walter Hassan. Ardenrun, the location of those fabled parties, burned down before the Second World War and Barnato died of cancer in July 1948 having married his third wife only a few months earlier; he was 52.

For Tim Birkin, the period after the Le Mans race of 1930 seemed to bode well – he took second place in the French Grand Prix at Pau driving a stripped-down, supercharged Bentley. Later that year he suffered a slight setback when Dorothy Paget withdrew her support. The Blowers were all sold, except one, which she kept and allowed Tim to race from time to time. Nevertheless, Tim continued to compete, albeit in foreign cars, and he won Le Mans in 1931 driving an Alfa Romeo with Lord Howe. He later recalled, 'I was thinking how much greater my satisfaction would have been in a Bentley instead of an Alfa-Romeo, when a telegram arrived from Mussolini, congratulating Francis Howe and myself on our success – "for Italy."'[277]

His finances, however, were not going anything like as well. He had gone into partnership with Mike Couper, a young motorcycle enthusiast, using his Welwyn works to hot up production cars, but this partnership quickly ran into trouble. Birkin also failed to succeed with a company called Miniature Speedways Ltd., for which the Welwyn works developed an early version of Scalextric called the 'Brooklands Race Game'.

In 1933 the racing season beckoned and he found support from his old companion from the Bentley days, Bernard Rubin. He and Rubin drove in the Mille Miglia. Rubin then entered Sir Henry Birkin (as he now was) in the Tripoli Grand Prix, where, in spite of poor pit work and strong rumours that the race had been fixed, he managed to finish third. But while filling up with oil he burnt both forearms on the hot exhaust.[278] A couple of weeks later he was back in London and, according to W.O., he even gave a summer party at Ciro's. However, he went down with flu-like symptoms and became rather listless. Benjafield was called and at first thought it was a bout of depression, but then noticed the small dressings on his arms, found out about the burns and wanted him admitted to a nursing home with blood poisoning.

In the end, Birkin agreed reluctantly. "If I do go in will you promise I will be out again in time for Nurburg?", he asked. "If you don't go in there is every possibility you will not get to Nurburg or any other race", warned Benjy darkly.[279] Sir Henry acquiesced to his old friend and was admitted to the Lady Caernarvon Clinic, where he died on the morning of 22 June.

But even though he died young, just a couple of years after the Bentley

CHAPTER TWENTY

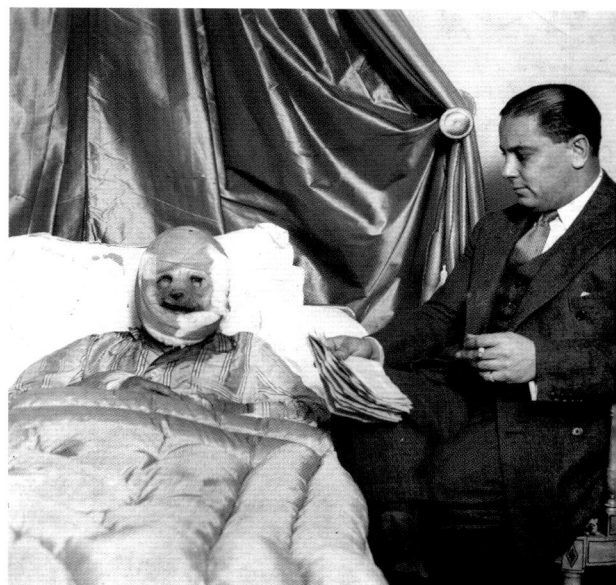

era had drawn to a close, Birkin had already outlived two of the Bentley Boys, who never even got to see middle age.

Glen Kidston had seemed indestructible, having been torpedoed in the war and survived the break up of his powerboat at speed. In Africa, pursuing his big-game hunting activities, he faced charges by both a wounded lion and a wounded rhino; the latter was shot dead at a distance of two yards. Driving in the Ulster T.T. of August 1928 he survived a crash at more than 95 m.p.h. However, his most spectacular escape came in 1929, when the passenger aircraft in which he was travelling crashed shortly after take off from Croydon. Recounting the experience, he told a *Daily Mail* reporter:

> I seemed to feel instinctively that we were going to crash. I can only attribute it to the fact that my long experience in flying and motor-racing has given me a sort of sixth sense. I put up my right hand to shield my eyes, and with left hand grasped some of the woodwork.
>
> The idea of fire flashed across my mind, and I next noticed fire breaking out forward. I saw a hole in the starboard side of the cabin and made for it. With an effort I wrenched myself through and was free of the tangled, burning mass.[280]

Kidston's clothes were on fire and, after he had rolled on the ground to extinguish the flames, he found he was quite badly burned. Nevertheless, he insisted on taking to the air for a short flight immediately after the accident to make sure that he did not lose his nerve. Only then did he take to his bed, bandaged like an Egyptian mummy. One of the inconveniences was that he 'could only get a cigarette to his lips by opening a hole in the wadding'.[281] Of course, his motor-racing friends rushed to see him, Benjy with his doctor's bag and Barnato with his good wishes. There is an

Kidston's Bentley skidded sensationally before crashing at Bradshaw's Brae (previous page) whilst competing in the 1929 T.T. at Ards, Ulster. The Autocar *reported that 'When Glen Kidston crashed in the big Bentley the car narrowly missed a telegraph pole; the driver was heard to remark afterwards that he had "never seen a telegraph pole move so quickly before."'*

Glen Kidston in front of his plane (above left), following his record-breaking flight from London to Cape Town.

Recovering after a plane crash in 1929, Kidston was confined to bedrest in his flat in Grosvenor Square (above right), but happily could accept visits from his Bentley cohorts.

evocative image of a bandaged Kidston propped up in bed while Barnato, holding what looks like a sheaf of telegrams from well-wishers, enjoys a cigarette at the patient's bedside.[282]

If anything, Kidston found aviation more rewarding than he did motor racing, even though he began taking flying lessons only towards the end of 1927. Personal aviation was a fad in the 1920s and among the Bentley Boys, Duller, Rubin and Birkin used to fly; but for Kidston it was more than an amusing pastime or a way to pick up women. "Flying is not as exciting as motoring, more particularly road racing", he once explained. "There you have the thrill of jockeying with the other drivers, cornering. In flying you just sit still for hours on end. But there is more to flying in the way of development. Motor racing is just sport."[283]

But although Kidston saw the commercial potential in flying, he still brought the same glamour to the skies that he had to the motor racing circuit: a photograph of him preparing to take off in a round-England air race shows him seated in the cockpit flirting with two pretty young women. Kidston was as fanatical about aeroplanes as Birkin was about motor racing; and as the dapper baronet felt that Britain was falling behind the world in motor racing, so Kidston believed Britain was missing valuable opportunities in the field of air transport.

In 1931 he determined to draw attention to the state of British aviation with a record-breaking flight from England to Cape Town. 'My object', he wrote in a letter to a friend, 'is to make our people wake up. In the commercial sphere we are miles behind!'[284] He covered the distance in six days and ten hours. The statement he issued on finishing his journey was simple. "If I can carry through a single trip like this as a private owner without proper organisation, it must stand to reason that a commercial company operating the same route with relays of machines should be able to do it much quicker."[285]

The British newspapers reacted with the same wild enthusiasm that they had shown when Kidston had won Le Mans the preceding year, and his achievement stirred up much controversy. While he was in South Africa, he decided to make an aerial tour of the country and, because the Lockheed-Vega in which he had made his record-breaking flight was too big for the majority of South African airstrips, he borrowed a Puss Moth for the purpose. On 5 May 1931 the afternoon papers in South Africa carried the following news in the 'Stop Press' column: 'Glen Kidston Reported Killed ... aeroplane crashed ... visiting-cards found nearby ... *Lieutenant Commander G. P. Glen Kidston*, R.N.'[286]

The names in their shirt collars and the signet ring on Kidston's finger, which had been given to him by his wife on the birth of their son Archie, proved the only form of identification because both the bodies of Kidston and his co-pilot were so mangled. The engine had been forced through the

CHAPTER TWENTY

Kidston brought the same glamour to the skies that he had to the motor racing circuit.

bodies on impact; of one corpse only the back of the head remained intact. An inquiry into the accident concluded that the plane was heavily laden and that when it encountered turbulence, unsecured luggage, in particular a typewriter case and camera left loose in a luggage rack, was thrown around the fuselage, damaging the aircraft.

The truly poignant part of the story is that, after years of loveless marriage, Kidston was in love with a beautiful young woman who later became Margaret, Duchess of Argyll. He had had numerous affairs, including one with a Hollywood actress, but this girl, to whom he had been introduced by Barnato, was different. They had been seen together for three months but he had, to use her term, been undemonstrative. Perhaps this had something do with her mother's rule that she could not dine alone with a man unless they had been seeing each other for a year. He had dropped her off at her hotel the night before his flight and sent a diamond watch from Cartier to her with a note explaining his feelings. On the day after he died she received a letter that said, 'Sweetheart I'm terribly in love with you. I never realised it until I got down here.'[287] News of Kidston's relationship with this young, beautiful debutante had reached his widow, who made it plain she did not want her husband's inamorata at the memorial service. But she went anyway, accompanied by Dale Bourne, who had driven with Barnato on the Blue Train run.

A couple of months later Kidston's widow was romantically linked to Edmund Sheffield, a Scunthorpe baronet's son, while Margaret became Duchess of Argyll and one of the most scandalous women of her generation. However, almost 50 years after Kidston's death, she said, 'I knew then, as I know now, that Glen Kidston was the man I should have married'. She still wore the Cartier watch he had left for her after their last dinner together.[288]

Kidston's red Puss Moth alongside his Bentley. This place was flown by Kidston in the 1930 King's Cup Air Race, an annual 800 mile race around Britain. Less than a year later it was in a Puss Moth that Kidston died whilst taking an aerial tour of South Africa.

THE GOLDEN YEARS

The 1930s saw the Bentley Boys either settling down or dying.

A selection of Sallon's cartoons, depicting various Bentley Boys. Clockwise, from top left: W.O., Kensington-Moir, Clement, Jack Dunfee, Davis and Benjy.

On 2 June Kidston's remains were buried at St Peter's Church in the Welsh town of Glasbury on Wye. His coffin was carried by a detachment of Boy Scouts instead of the usual gloomy pallbearers, 'Rule Britannia' was sung at the service as he had wished, and the floral tribute from his mother was a large cross of the white heather that he had so loved as a young boy.

Just as tragic was the death of Clive Dunfee at Brooklands in 1932. After Bentley was absorbed into Rolls-Royce the Dunfees continued to drive Barnato's Bentleys at Brooklands. For the 500 Miles race of 1932 Barnato had entered Old No.1, the car in which he and Kidston had won Le Mans. Since then the car had been fitted with an 8-litre engine. Clive Dunfee had married actress Jane Baxter in December 1930 and, as seems to have been part of the marriage vows at the time, promised not to race again. However his wife gave him a dispensation to drive with his brother in this race; after all, it included Clive's three favourite 'B's: Bentley, Barnato and Brooklands. But Clive was not used to the car and had not raced in more than a year.

The race had been going well for the first two and half hours when Jack came into the pits to hand over to his brother. Tyres changed and the car refuelled, the two brothers shook hands, then Clive took the big Bentley back out on the track where it was soon lapping at over 120 m.p.h. But a short time later, while overtaking another car on the banking, Clive lost control of the car and was killed. The report in *The Motor* captures those last seconds of his life as he struggled to keep the big heavy car on the track as it scraped along the lip of the banking:

> As he approached the Members' Bridge, spectators were horrified to see that one wheel was actually over the edge of the banking, chipping pieces out of the trees as the car hurtled past. For a moment it seemed that Dunfee had got the car under control; then, hitting a pine tree with such force that it was cut in half and flung on to the track, the great Bentley turned broadside on, doing a double roll in mid-air, and flinging its occupant on to the edge of the track, killing him instantly. The car vanished through the trees, razing them to the ground for a width of several feet, and finished down the steep bank on the private road below, a total wreck. Mrs Clive Dunfee, who was in the Bentley pit at the time of the accident, hurried to the scene, whither Capt. Woolf Barnato, the entrant, was taken in the Stewards' Car.[289]

Old No.1 was repaired and, bodied by Mulliner as a fixed-head coupé, went on a 10,000 mile tour of America as a sort of extended honeymoon for Barnato and his second wife, Jacqueline Claridge Quealy. But Jack Dunfee never raced again.

The 1930s saw the Bentley Boys either settling down or dying … or, in the case of Bernard Rubin, both. Rubin married in 1935 and in the summer of 1936, shortly after setting himself up as an English country squire with a house called Old Cloth Hall, he died, aged 39.

CHAPTER TWENTY

John Duff had left England for Los Angeles in 1926, where he had opened a fencing school – he was as talented with a foil as with a racing car. The same year that he won Le Mans he was selected for the British fencing squad at the Olympic Games and he was Gary Cooper's double in the sword-fighting sequences of *Beau Geste*. He retuned to England in the 1930s, bred horses and became a noted show jumper. He died in 1958, breaking his neck when he was thrown from a horse.

In the 1950s surviving Bentley Boys, among them the portly *bon vivants* Dr Benjafield and Bertie Kensington Moir, Frank Clement, Sammy Davis, Jack Dunfee, Earl Howe, the Duke of Richmond and Gordon and W.O. Bentley were included in a gallery of prominent racing drivers drawn by Sallon to commemorate the 60th anniversary of the British Motor Industry.

Benjy lived to be 69, continuing his medical practice and his interest in motor sport. He raced ERA R6B at Donington in the mid-thirties, sharing the driving with Earl Howe. In 1957, exactly thirty years after the White House Crash victory at Le Mans, he died at home in Harley Street.[290]

The Bentley Girls survived well into the second half of the twentieth century: the monumental Dorothy Paget achieved fame as a heavy backer and breeder of horses. One of her greatest successes was a horse called 'Golden Miller', which won the Cheltenham Gold Cup five times in succession between 1932 and 1936.

Her turf record combined with her increasing eccentricity made her a celebrity in the drab years endured by Britain after the Second World War. Her existence became nocturnal; it was probably to avoid seeing too many people that she lived her life the wrong way round, eating breakfast at 6.30p.m., taking a heavy lunch at around 10p.m. and then dining in the

early morning. At night she conducted business relating to her passion for horse racing. However, she still kept fast cars, driving them at alarming speed with little regard for traffic lights and the like if she happened to be late for race meetings. In the last period of her life she favoured Jaguars.

Paget became a thoroughly British riposte to Howard Hughes; among her many quirks was the one of assigning various secretaries colours instead of using their names. She also took to issuing detailed memoranda on almost every aspect of her life, including visits to the lavatory. 'She sometimes sends out a note telling "all colours" except blue that she is going to the loo', wrote one young secretary home to her mother. 'Blue is Mrs Robbins, who lives in London, and I suppose Miss P. thinks she would be finished before Mrs Robbins got the message. Miss P. is very preoccupied with the loo, and if she doesn't go she thinks she is going to die, and sends for the doctor.'[291]

Dorothy Paget's gluttonous, nocturnal existence finally exacted its toll in February 1960, when she died of heart failure brought on by her massive weight. She bequeathed her 75 horses to her sister. A friend wrote to *The Times* saying, 'She was neither beautiful nor intelligent, but she was kind and generous.'[292]

After her record at Montlhéry, the Hon. Mrs Victor Bruce took to the sea to break some powerboat records, and at the end of one rapid cross-Channel jaunt she told reporters that, "In future when I want to cross the Channel I shall use my speedboat instead of the Channel steamers, which are push-carts by comparison."[293] She then bought a plane, took up flying, broke some more records, joined a flying circus, started a business called Air Dispatch, ran a factory repairing downed R.A.F. aircraft during the war, made a million pounds and, aged 81, took a refresher course in flying and looped the loop over Bristol. She finally died in 1989, aged 94.

The first of the Bentley Boys, Sammy Davis, boyhood friend of W.O. Bentley, was also the last. A serious accident in 1931 had threatened to end Davis' racing career, but he continued to compete as a rally driver and frequently entered the Monte Carlo rally. He founded the Veteran Car Club of Great Britain and was made an honorary citizen of Le Mans, where a street was named after him. He continued to work as a motoring journalist, writing the obituaries of many of the Bentley Boys. He died in January 1981, on his 94th birthday.

Glen Kidston best summed up the spirit of the Bentley Boys: shortly before he left for South Africa on his fatal trip he scribbled a few sentences about how he would like his funeral arranged. The first two paragraphs serve as a fitting epitaph for this unique group of men from a unique time.

> If I die, I don't want no regrets. [sic] I've had a good run for my money and I'll die quite content.
>
> I don't want no maudlin sentiment or sob stuff — just say, everyone, he's had a good show and tried to do his bit. I want nothing more.[294]

The body of Glen Kidston and that of his co-pilot lie side by side, April 1931.

Epilogue

The winning Bentley Speed 8 of the 2003 Le Mans, accompanied by two Blowers, bring Paris to a standstill during their victory parade down the Champs Elysee.

Sammy Davis certainly had a good show, but it is difficult not to wish that he had lived a little longer. Had he survived until March 1982 he would have seen the beginning of the revival of Bentley's fortunes.

Ever since the acquisition of the marque by Rolls-Royce, Bentley's identity had been eroded. By the late 1950s Bentleys were little more than badge-engineered Rolls-Royces, and come the end of the 1970s Rolls-Royce production outnumbered Bentley by twenty to one.

Then, at the Geneva Motor Salon of 1982, the Bentley Mulsanne Turbo was launched: at least half as powerful again as the Rolls-Royce, it immediately revived the fortunes of the winged 'B'. The 1980s and '90s saw ever-faster Bentleys and a commensurate increase in sales. By the time Rolls-Royce and Bentley parted company in 1998 – the former coming under the ownership of B.M.W., the latter purchased by the Volkswagen Group – Bentleys were selling at four times the rate of Rolls-Royces.

The period subsequent to the takeover by the German car group proved to be one of the most dynamic since the company was founded. During a period of investment and financial stability – a new experience for the marque – Bentley was able to realise the potential that its devotees have always known existed. Under its new owners, Bentley

EPILOGUE

> The most emotional act in the restoration of Bentley, was its return to Le Mans.

Evoking the spirit of Bentleys Le Mans glory days, Leitzinger, van de Poele and Wallace take to the podium wearing Twenties-style overalls.

finally became what it could have been had the financial crisis of the 1930s not intervened.

A new car, the Continental G.T., was launched in 2003, providing a sporty sibling to the majestic and powerful four-door Arnage, which itself underwent almost constant upgrading and aesthetic improvement during the early twenty-first century. The launch of the Continental G.T. was followed by another four door, The Flying Spur, a high-speed saloon sharing the look of the G.T. and capable of nudging 200m.p.h. Then in 2006 the first new model convertibles appeared on the road: the Azure, a stately two-door drophead modelled on the Arnage and a smaller (a relative term at Bentley) convertible version of the Continental G.T.

However the most emotional act in the restoration of Bentley, was its return to Le Mans. Even through the firm's less successful years, vintage Bentleys retained their special link with Le Mans and quite properly the V.W. Group decided that if it was to return Bentley to its position as a maker of unique cars combining luxury, pedigree and sporting capabilities, it needed to show that it could win at Le Mans like it used to in the Twenties.

Bentley returned to Le Mans with a works team in 2001 and made it to the podium finishing in third position and then in a theatrical touch which delighted the crowds, the team of Leitzinger, van de Poele and Lawrence appeared in front of the crowds in 1920s style white belted overalls, goggles and helmets which would have been familiar to the original Bentley Boys.

And in 2003 Team Bentley won Le Mans almost three quarters of a century after Birkin's Blowers had harried Carraciola's Mercedes and Barnato and Kidston had driven to Bentley's epic 1930 victory. A victory parade of Bentleys rolled down the Champs Elysees and on June 18th, the historic dinner at the Savoy was recreated to celebrate this historic win. At this dinner there were two guests of honour, the winning Speed 8, car No. 7, and Diana Barnato Walker, daughter of the quondam chairman.

Le Mans…The Savoy… Bentley was, at last, back where it belonged: where it had been during the Roaring Twenties, when Bentley Boys built the legend of the winged 'B'.

Notes

CHAPTER 1

1. Bentley, Walter Owen, *W.O. An Autobiography*, Hutchinson & Co., London, 1961, p.91
2. Hillstead, Arthur F.C., *Those Bentley Days*, Faber & Faber, London, 1953, p.30
3. *Ibid*, p.30
4. Pennal, quoted in Nagle, Elizabeth, *The Other Bentley Boys*, George G. Harrup & Co. Ltd, London, 1964, p.31
5. Hillstead, *Those Bentley Days*, p.30
6. Benzole was a more efficacious propellant than the petrol of the day.
7. *Ibid*, p.30
8. *Ibid*, p.31
9. Pennal, quoted in Nagle, *The Other Bentley Boys*, p.31
10. *Ibid*, pp.31–2
11. Bentley, *W.O. An Autobiography*, p.91
12. *Ibid*, p.91
13. *Ibid*, p.91
14. Pennal, quoted in Nagle, *The Other Bentley Boys*, p.32
15. *Ibid*, p.32

CHAPTER 2

16. Bentley, *W.O. An Autobiography*, p.91
17. *Ibid*, p.14
18. *Ibid*, p.37
19. *Ibid*, p.51
20. *Ibid*, p.52
21. Advertisement reproduced in Frankel, Andrew, *Bentley, The Story*, Redwood Publishing Ltd, London, 2003, p.19
22. Hillstead, Arthur F.C., *Fifty Years with Motor Cars*, Faber & Faber, London, 1960, p.98
23. Bentley, *W.O. An Autobiography*, p.92
24. Original letter reproduced in Hay, Michael, *Bentley Factory Cars 1919–1931*, Osprey Publishing, Oxford, 1998, p.41
25. Hassan, Walter, with Graham Robson, *Climax in Coventry: My Life of Fine Engines and Fast Cars*, Mercian Manuals, Coventry, 1997, p.11

CHAPTER 3

26. Hay, *Bentley Factory Cars 1919–1931*, p.116
27. *Ibid*, p.145
28. Davis, S.C.H., *A Racing Motorist: His Adventures at the Wheel in Peace and War*, Iliffe & Sons, Ltd, London, 1949, p.211
29. *Ibid*, p.211
30. Davis quoted in Allen, Sir Peter, *Transport Pioneers of the Twentieth Century*, Patrick Stevens for The Transport Trust, Cambridge, 1981, p.2
31. Davis, *A Racing Motorist: His Adventures at the Wheel in Peace and War*, p.9
32. *Ibid*, pp.9–10
33. *Ibid*, p.10
34. Davis, S.C.H., *Motor Racing*, Iliffe & Sons, Ltd, London, 1932, p.54
35. *Ibid*, p.54
36. Davis, *A Racing Motorist: His Adventures at the Wheel in Peace and War*, p.15
37. *The Autocar*, 29 November 1919
38. Letter to Peter Holmes, 16 February 1985, Bentley Drivers' Club Archives
39. Bentley, *W.O. An Autobiography*, p.97
40. S.C.H. Davis quoted in *Bentley Drivers' Club Review*, No. 140, May 1981, p.87
41. *The Autocar*, 24 January 1920
42. Bentley, *W.O. An Autobiography*, p.97

CHAPTER 4

43. *The Autocar*, 27 August 1921
44. Hillstead, *Fifty Years with Motor Cars*, pp.119–20
45. *Ibid*, p.166
46. Bentley, *W.O. An Autobiography*, p.100
47. Hassan, *Climax in Coventry*, p.11
48. *The Autocar*, 27 August 1921
49. Bentley, *W.O. An Autobiography*, p.101
50. *Ibid*, p.101
51. *Ibid*, p.101
52. Hillstead, *Those Bentley Days*, p.50
53. *The Autocar*, 1 October 1921
54. Pennal quoted in Nagle, *The Other Bentley Boys*, pp.59–60
55. Pennal, *ibid*, p.60
56. Hillstead, *Fifty Years with Motor Cars*, p.127
57. *Ibid*, p.127

CHAPTER 5

58. Davis, quoted in Allen, *Pioneers of Transport*, pp.6–7
59. Hillstead, *Fifty Years with Motor Cars*, p.33
60. *The Motor*, quoted in Hillstead, *Those Bentley Days*, p.49
61. *The Autocar*, quoted in *ibid*, p.50
62. *The Motor*, quoted in *ibid*, p.50
63. Hillstead, *Those Bentley Days*, pp.51–2
64. *Ibid*, p.53
65. *Ibid*, p.52
66. Hillstead, *Fifty Years with Motor Cars*, p.128
67. *Ibid*, p.169
68. *Ibid*, p.169
69. Hillstead, *Those Bentley Days*, p.53

CHAPTER 6

70. *The Autocar*, 17 June 1922, quoted in Hay, *Bentley Factory Cars 1919–1931*, p.104
71. Berthon, Darell, *A Racing History of the Bentley (1921–31)*, The Bodley Head, London, 1956, p.17
72. Bentley, *W.O. An Autobiography*, p.106
73. Quoted in Hillstead, *Those Bentley Days*, p.61
74. Quoted in *ibid*, p.62
75. Manuscript by Herbert Kensington Moir, 16 May 1990, Bentley Drivers' Club Archives
76. Bentley, *W.O. An Autobiography*, p.107
77. *Ibid*, p.107
78. Saunders quoted in Nagle, *The Other Bentley Boys*, p.75
79. W.O. maintains that the dog was a 'Blenheim spaniel'.
80. Saunders quoted in *ibid*, p.75
81. Saunders quoted in *ibid*, p.153

CHAPTER 7

82. Fletcher, Rivers, *Bentley Past and Present*, Gentry Books Ltd., 1982, p.27
83. Bentley, *W.O. An Autobiography*, p.115
84. Clement quoted in Nagle, *The Other Bentley Boys*, p.92
85. Andrews quoted in *Bentley Drivers' Club Review*, No. 232, April 2004, p.100
86. Hassan quoted in Nagle, *The Other Bentley Boys*, p.83
87. Pennal quoted in *ibid*, p.83
88. Andrews quoted in *Bentley Drivers' Club Review*, No. 232, April 2004, p.100
89. Pennal quoted in Nagle, *The Other Bentley Boys*, p.88

CHAPTER 8

90. Bentley, *W.O. An Autobiography*, p.116
91. Quoted in Nagle, *The Other Bentley Boys*, p.83
92. Bentley, *W.O. An Autobiography*, p.116
93. *Ibid*, p.116
94. Hillstead, *Those Bentley Days*, p.94
95. *Ibid*, p.94
96. Bentley, *W.O. An Autobiography*, p.117
97. *Ibid*, p.117
98. *The Autocar*, June 1 1923

CHAPTER 9

99. Manuscript by Dr. J.D. Benjafield, 'The British Racing Driver's Club 1927–52', Bentley Drivers' Club Archive, p.3

100 *Bentley Drivers' Club Review*, No. 3, December 1946, p.2
101 *Ibid*, p.2
102 Manuscript by Dr. J.D. Benjafield, 'The British Racing Driver's Club 1927–52', Bentley Drivers' Club Archive, p.3
103 *Ibid*, p.3
104 *Ibid*, p.3
105 *Bentley Drivers' Club Review*, No. 3, December 1946, p.3
106 *Ibid*, p.3
107 *Ibid*, p.4
108 *Ibid*, p.4
109 *Ibid*, p.4–5
110 *Ibid*, p.5
111 *Ibid*, p.5
112 Manuscript by Dr. J.D. Benjafield, 'The British Racing Driver's Club 1927–52', Bentley Drivers' Club Archive, p.5
113 *Bentley Drivers' Club Review*, No. 3, December 1946, p.7
114 *Ibid*, pp.7–8
115 Bob Benjafield, editorial comment

CHAPTER 10

116 Hay, *Bentley Factory Cars 1919–1931*, p.144
117 Hillstead, *Fifty Years with Motor Cars*, p.148
118 *Ibid*, p.148
119 *Ibid*, p.148
120 *Ibid*, p.146
121 Bentley, *W.O. An Autobiography*, p.111

CHAPTER 11

122 *Bentley Drivers' Club Review*, No. 169, August 1988, p.165
123 Emden, Paul H., *Randlords – An Account of the Pioneers of the Witwatersrand Diamond and Gold Mines*, Hodder & Stoughton, London, 1935, p.123
124 *Ibid*, p.123
125 Roberts, Brian, *The Diamond Magnates*, Hamish Hamilton Ltd, London, 1972, p.228
126 *Ibid*, p.228
127 *Ibid*, p.234
128 *Ibid*, p.235
129 Jackson, Stanley, *The Great Barnato*, Heinemann, London, 1970, p.261
130 Bentley, *W.O. An Autobiography*, p.151
131 *Ibid*, p.152
132 Barnato's daughter Diana explained that he always asked people to fill their cases from a large cigarette box instead, so that he wasn't continually emptying his case.
133 Hillstead, *Fifty Years with Motor Cars*, p.150

CHAPTER 12

134 Davis, *Motor Racing*, p.81
135 *Ibid*, p.84
136 Bentley, *W.O. An Autobiography*, p.141
137 *Ibid*, p.141
138 *Ibid*, p.154
139 *Ibid*, p.154
140 *Sporting Life*, 19 May 1926
141 Hillstead, *Those Bentley Days*, p.132
142 *Daily Mail*, 18 May 1926
143 *Ibid*.
144 S.C.H. Davis in *The Autocar*, 17 August 1962, p.277
145 *South Wales News*, 18 January 1928
146 *Evening News*, 19 May 1926
147 *Star*, 29 January 1926

CHAPTER 13

148 Bentley, *W.O. An Autobiography*, p.155
149 *Ibid*, p.155
150 *Ibid*, p.135
151 Davis, *Great British Drivers*, p.32
152 *Ibid*, p.32
153 Fletcher, *Bentley Past and Present*, p.36
154 Argyll, Margaret Campbell, *Forget Not: The Autobiography of Margaret, Duchess of Argyll*, W.H. Allen, London, p.50
155 'Sales of the 3 Litre fell away to almost nothing after the introduction of the 4½ Litre'. Hay, Michael, *Bentley Factory Cars 1919–1931*, p.340.
156 Fletcher, *Bentley Past and Present*, pp.87–9
157 *Ibid*, p.87
158 Jackson, *The Great Barnato*, p.261
159 Bentley, *W.O. An Autobiography*, p.114
160 Fletcher, *Bentley Past and Present*, p.27
161 Jack Dunfee, son of a City financier, was a friend of Barnato's and a noted racing driver.
162 *Ibid*, pp.75–7

CHAPTER 14

163 Davis, *Great British Racing Drivers*, pp.31–2
164 Bentley, *W.O. An Autobiography*, p.132
165 *Ibid*, p.132
166 'For some time no action was taken, due to a mistaken idea that Barnato was not a good enough driver to race Bentleys on Brooklands.' A.F.C. Hillstead, *Fifty Years with Motor Cars*, p.150
167 *Ibid*, p.133
168 Davis, *Motor Racing*, p.94
169 *Ibid*, p.108
170 Bentley, *W.O. An Autobiography*, p.159
171 Nagle, *The Other Bentley Boys*, p.115
172 *Ibid*, pp.115–16
173 Davis, *Motor Racing*, p.110
174 *Ibid*, p.285
175 *Ibid*, p.286
176 *Ibid*, p.110
177 *Ibid*, p.112
178 *Ibid*, p.112
179 Amherst Villiers quoted in *Classic and Sportscar*, August 1983, p.34
180 Quoted in Nagle, *The Other Bentley Boys*, p.137
181 Birkin Bart, Sir Henry 'Tim', *Full Throttle*, G.T. Foulis & Co. Ltd, London, pp.80–1
182 Davis, *Great British Drivers*, p.40
183 Birkin, *Full Throttle*, p.28
184 *Automobile Quarterly*, Spring 1968, p.371
185 Davis, *Great British Drivers*, p.40
186 Davis, *Motor Racing*, p.121
187 *Ibid*, p.122

CHAPTER 15

188 Davis, *Motor Racing*, p.127
189 *Automobile Quarterly*, Spring 1968, p.368
190 Davis, *Motor Racing*, p.129
191 *Ibid*, p.121
192 *The Motor*, reproduced in Bentley Le Mans brochure, p.4
193 *The Autocar*, reproduced in Bentley Le Mans brochure, p.12
194 *Daily Mail*, 20 June 1927, reproduced in Bentley Le Mans brochure
195 *The Tatler*, 29 June 1927, reproduced in Bentley Le Mans brochure
196 Davis, *Motor Racing*, p.135
197 Davis, *Casque's Sketch Book*, p.37
198 *The Autocar*, 1 July 1927
199 Davis, *Great British Racing Drivers*, p.33
200 *Ibid*, p.33

CHAPTER 16

201 Rivers Fletcher, however, does talk of visiting Barnato at Grosvenor House
202 Davis, *Motor Racing*, p.160
203 Saunders quoted in Nagle, *The Other Bentley Boys*, p.134
204 Davis, *Motor Racing*, p.207
205 Birkin, *Full Throttle*, p.93
206 Clement quoted in Nagle, *The Other Bentley Boys*, p.128
207 *Ibid*, p.129
208 Hassan quoted in *ibid*, pp.130–1
209 Saunders quoted in *ibid*, p.134
210 Clarke quoted in *ibid*, p.137
211 Clarke quoted in *ibid*, p.137

NOTES

212 Davis, *Motor Racing*, p.104
213 Quoted in Nagle, *The Other Bentley Boys*, p.132
214 Quoted in *ibid*, p.134
215 Bentley, *W.O. An Autobiography*, p.134
216 Quoted in Nagle, *The Other Bentley Boys*, p.137
217 Clarke's recollection is slightly confused; Birkin only succeeded to the baronetcy in 1931, so the woman is unlikely to have referred to him as "Sir" Henry.
218 Quoted in Nagle, *The Other Bentley Boys*, p.137

CHAPTER 17

219 Emily Davidson, who threw herself under the King's horse at the 1913 Derby and died of her injuries.
220 Quoted in Bullock, John, *Fast Women: The Drivers Who Changed the Face of Motor Racing*, Robson Books, London, 2002, p.50
221 Bruce, The Hon. Mrs Victor, *Nine Lives Plus – Record-breaking on Land, Sea and in the Air*, Pelham Books, London, 1977, p.81
222 *Ibid*, p.83
223 *Ibid*, pp.84–5
224 Bullock, *Fast Women*, p.48
225 Saunders quoted in Nagle, *The Other Bentley Boys*, p.172
226 Bruce, *Nine Lives Plus*, p.85
227 *Ibid*, p.86
228 *Ibid*, p.92
229 *Bentley Drivers' Club Review*, No. 148, May 1983, p.120
230 Gilbey, Quintin, *Queen of the Turf – The Dorothy Paget Story*, Arthur Barker Ltd, 1974, p.10
231 *Ibid*, p.56
232 Bentley, *W.O. An Autobiography*, p.174
233 Nagle, *The Other Bentley Boys*, p.193
234 *Sporting Life*, quoted in Gilbey, *Queen of the Turf – The Dorothy Paget Story*, p.106
235 *Ibid*, p.12
236 Birkin, *Full Throttle*, p.94
237 *Ibid*, p.95
238 *Ibid*, pp.95–6
239 *Ibid*, p.101
240 *Ibid*, p.102
241 *Ibid*, p.80
242 *Sporting Life*, quoted in Gilbey, *Queen of the Turf – The Dorothy Paget Story*, p.106
243 *Ibid*, p.13

CHAPTER 18

244 *The Times*, 6 March 1930
245 *Ibid*
246 Nagle, *The Other Bentley Boys*, p.180
247 *Bentley Bedside Book*, p.2
248 *Ibid*, p.2
249 *Ibid*, pp.2–3
250 In his article 'The Bentley Formerly Known as The Blue Train Car' (*Bentley Drivers' Club Review*, February 2002) pp.26–31, makes it clear that the Gurney Nutting coupé could not have been the Blue Train Car because it was finished only towards the end of May 1930, two months after the run had been completed. Instead, 'it is almost certainly the case that the real Blue Train Bentley is UU5999 chassis BA2592 delivered new to Woolf Barnato on 19 June 1929 with four door four-light Weymann saloon coachwork by H.J. Mulliner'. In his own account, Barnato talks of the car he used as 'my Saloon Speed Six' not a coupé. A rich American bought the Gurney Nutting coupé and when he discovered it was not the Blue Train car, made enquiries and purchased the real Blue Train Bentley as well.
251 *Ibid*, p.3
252 Diana Barnato Walker, editorial comment

CHAPTER 19

253 Carraciola, Rudolf, *A Racing Driver's World*, Motoraces Book Club, London, 1963, p.1
254 *Ibid*, p.47
255 Birkin, *Full Throttle*, p.47
256 *Ibid*, p.52
257 Bentley, *W.O. An Autobiography*, pp.175–6
258 Benjafield, J.D., *The Bentleys at Le Mans*, Motor Racing Publications, Abingdon, 1948, p.33
259 *Ibid*, p.32
260 The green-and-blue tie was given by W.O. to those drivers who finished a race, while anyone who drove a Blower could wear the red-and-grey; the result was that Benjy was entitled to wear both and, in the words of Sammy Davis, 'always came to the right party with the wrong tie!' (*Motor Racing*, p.251)
261 Davis, *Motor Racing*, p.250
262 *Ibid*, pp.252–3
263 *Ibid*, p.253
264 *Ibid*, p.254
265 W.O. says it was a blown gasket but Davis and *The Motor* both cite electrics: 'According to Mr. Neubauer, the head of the racing department, this sudden discharging of the battery was due to a short circuit in the dynamo'. *The Motor*, 24 June 1930
266 Berthon, *A Racing History of the Bentley*, p.103
267 Bentley, *W.O. An Autobiography*, p.177
268 Hay, *Bentley Factory Cars 1919–1931*, p.310
269 *The Sketch*, 27 August 1930
270 *Bystander*, 27 August 1930
271 *Evening Standard*, 25 August 1930

CHAPTER 20

272 Benjafield, *The Bentleys at Le Mans*, pp.39–40
273 Piers Brendon
274 Manuscript by Glen Kidston to Home Kidston, 30 August 1930, Kidston family archive
275 Manuscript by Glen Kidston to Margaret Duchess of Argyll, 22 April 1931, Kidston family archive, quoted in Argyll, *Forget Not*, p.55
276 Bentley, *W.O. An Autobiography*, p.153
277 Birkin, *Full Throttle*, p.113
278 According to W.O. Birkin burnt his arm on the exhaust 'while reaching into the cockpit to retrieve his cigarette-lighter.' Bentley, *W.O. An Autobiography*, p.126
279 Davis, *Great British Drivers*, p.47
280 Glen Kidston, quoted in the *Daily Mail*, 7 August 1929
281 *Daily Mail*, 7 August 1929
282 *Star*, 7 November 1929, and *Daily Mirror*, 8 November 1929
283 Quoted in Bennett, Benjamin, *Down Africa's Skyways*, Hutchinson & Co., London, 1932, p.190
284 Letter to Esmonde Phillips, 22 March 1931, Bentley Drivers' Club Archive
285 Quoted in Bennett, *Down Africa's Skyways*, p.199
286 *Ibid*, p.207
287 Argyll, *Forget Not*, p.57
288 *Ibid*, p.58
289 *The Motor*, quoted in Hay, Michael, *Bentley "Old Number One"*, Number One Press, Devon, 1999, p.83
290 Bob Benjafield, editorial comment
291 Quoted in Gilbey, *Queen of the Turf – The Dorothy Paget Story*, p.122
292 Hutchings, quoted in *Brooklands Society Gazette*, Vol.28, No.1
293 Quoted in Bullock, *Fast Women*, p.49
294 Manuscript in Kidston family archive, n.d.

Index

Figures in *italics* refer to captions

A

A.C. (car) *54*, 136, 139
Adlington, William 56
aircraft
  Bentley engines *20*, 21
  Puss Moths 163, 174, *175*
  Sopwith Camels *20*, 22
Alfa Romeo 172
Ambassador Club, London 90
Amherst Villiers 142
Ardenrun Place, nr Lingfield, Surrey 77, 78–9, *79*, *81*, 81–2, *83*, 85
  basement pub 96
  destroyed by fire 172
  'farewell-to-motor racing' party (1930) 163
  improvised racing circuit 96
  victory party (for Le Mans, 1920) 132, *132*
  weekend parties 97
Ardenrun V (powerboat) 102
Ards circuit, Northern Ireland (1929) 154
Argyll, Margaret, Duchess of 175
Astaire, Fred 98
Aston, Captain Wilfred Gordon 118
Aston Clinton Hill Climb 21
Aston Martins *13*, 42, 49
Autocar, The 30, 33, 34, 36, 65, 118, 131

B

Bankhead, Tallulah 98
Barnato, Barney (Barnett Isaacs) 82–4
Barnato, Fanny (née Bees) 83, 84
Barnato, Jack 83, 84
Barnato, Jacqueline (née Quealy) 169, 176
Barnato, June (née Howard-Tripp) 98, *98*
Barnato, Leah 84
Barnato, Woolf
  appearance 84, 98
  at Ardenrun 79, 96, *see* Ardenrun Place
  and W.O. Bentley 85, 96, 102, 166
  and Bentley Motors takeover 88–9, *89*, 94–6, 104
  as Bentley owner 97, 98, 148
  and Birkin's Blowers 156, 157
  birth and childhood 83, 84
  Blue Train run 149–51
  Brooklands (1921) 42
  Brooklands (1927) 105
  and The Hon. Mrs Victor Bruce 138
  at Cambridge 84
  character and personality 85, 97–8, 101–2, 104, 119, 148
  'cocktail' racing 163
  death 172
  forms 'Brooklands Squad' 90, *91*
  founds Ambassador Club 90
  and Hillstead's visit to Ardenrun 77, 85
  Le Mans (1925) 88
  Le Mans (1927) *25*, 109, 110, 119, *119*
  Le Mans (1928) 127, *127*
  Le Mans (1929) *125*, 128, 132, *132*
  Le Mans (1930) 74, 156, 157, 159, *160*, 162, *162*
  loses money on Bentley Motors 169, 172
  love of Riviera 148, 163
  marriages *see* wives (*below*)
  powerboat racing at Hendon (1931) 102
  and record-breaking attempt at Montlhéry (1926) 102
  and Rubin 125
  shooting at Shadwell 163
  visits Kidston after aircrash *173*, 173–4
  wagers 96, 102, 107, *see also* Blue Train run (*above*)
  war service 84
  withdraws Bentley Motors from motor racing 162, *162*–3
  wives 85, 98, *98*, 169, 172, 176
  and women 84, 96–7, 98, *see also* wives (*above*)
Beaumont, Mrs Louis 163
Belfast T.T. (1929) 156
Benjafield, Dr J. Dudley ('Benjy') 68, *70*, 128
  on Bentley Motor's withdrawal from racing 165
  as Birkin's doctor 172
  Brooklands (1927) 105
  as butt of jokes 96, 132
  cartoon of *176*, 177
  death 177
  Essex Six Hour (1928) 125
  as first 'Bentley Boy' 26, 68–71
  Le Mans (1925) 87, 88
  Le Mans (1926) 102
  Le Mans (1927) *25*, 109, 110, 116–17, 118–19
  Le Mans (1928) 127
  Le Mans (1929) *125*
  Le Mans (1930) 159, *159*
  and Montlhéry record attempt 102
  on supercharged Bentleys 156
  visits injured Kidston 173
Bentley, A.W. 18
Bentley, Colonel Horace Milner (H.M.)
  at Bentley & Bentley 12, 21, 22
  and Bentley Motors' financial problems 44, 75
  and Hillstead 43, 44
  as motorcycle rider 18, 30
  resigns 88–9
Bentley, Leonie 14, 21
Bentley, Walter Owen (W.O.) 6, *12*, *14*, *168*
  appearance 12
  apprenticeship on Great Northern Railway 18, *18*
  and Barnato's takeover of the company 77, 85, 88–9, 94–5, 96, 102, 166
  Belfast T.T. (1929) 156
  and Bentley Motors as club 35, 42–3
  and Bentley Motors' financial problems 44, 47, 76, 77
  and The Hon Mrs Victor Bruce 136, 138
  cartoon of 177
  character and personality 12, 17, 30, 76–7, 98
  childhood 18
  and Davis 30, 31
  death 169
  develops six-cylinder Bentleys 73, 75
  and D.F.P. sports cars *18*, 21, 22, *23*
  dog 51
  and early Brooklands races 41–2
  expertise as engineer 12, 166
  and first 3-litre Bentley 12–15, *15*, 22
  and first Bentley customer 34–6
  first competitive race 21
  initial opposition to Le Mans 24-hour races 61, 62
  Isle of Man T.T. (1922) 42, *43*, 44, 48–9, *49*
  at Lagonda 169
  Le Mans (1923) 64–5
  Le Mans (1924) 76
  Le Mans (1925) 88, 109
  Le Mans (1927) 25, 109, 110, 117
  Le Mans (1929) 127, 128–9, 130–31
  Le Mans (1930) 156
  Le Mans (1939) 169
  marketing genius 35, 36, 166–7
  marriage 21
  meets 'Bertie' Moir 49, 51
  and motorcycle racing 18, *18*
  removal as Managing Director of Bentley Motors 169
  at Rolls-Royce 169

187

INDEX

and supercharged Bentleys
(Blowers) 142, 156
views on speed 127, 154, 159
on withdrawing from motor racing
163
and women in the pits 130–31
in World War I 21–2
writes autobiography (1958) 17, 30, 76–7, 89,
98
Bentley & Bentley 21–2
see Bentley Motors Ltd
'Bentley Boys' 6–7, 51, 127–8, 165, 166–9
cartoons of 176, 177
and drink 129–30
first 26
and women 130–31
Bentley Motors Ltd 22, 33, 128
Cricklewood factory 34, 34, 35,
36, 69
financial difficulties 43, 44, 47, 75, 76–7, 163
first customer 34–6
first victory 42
showroom (No. 3 Hanover Court) 34
taken over by Rolls-Royce 169
withdrawal from motor racing 162–3, 165
see also Bentleys
Bentley Rotary One aero engine 21, 22
Bentley Rotary Two aero engine 20, 21
Bentleys
3-litre 12, 12–15, 15, 22, 30–31, 34,
41–2, 54, 56, 74, 75
4½-litre 108, 109, 110, 125, 136,
136, 142, see also Birkin's Blowers (below)
6½-litre 73, 75, 77, 85
8-litre 169
Arnage 167, 182
The Azure 182
Birkin's Blowers 109, 142, 142, 144, 156, 157,
159, 172, 181
Continental G.T. 182
EXP1 15
EXP2 41–2
The Flying Spur 182
Mulsanne 167, 181
Old No.7 102, 105, 109, 110, 112, 116, 117, 118,
119, 127, 176, 182
Speed Sixes 130, 149–51, 159, 159, 160
Speed Eight 181
Berthon, Darell: A Racing History of the Bentley
162
Birkin, Audrey (née Lathan) 105
Birkin, Charles Archibald 109
Birkin, (Sir) Henry Ralph Stanley
('Tim') 105

appearance and driving ensemble 107, 107, 144
and Barnato 105, 107
Belfast T.T. (1929) 156
Bentley début 105
Blowers see under Bentleys
breaks Brooklands lap record 107
at Brooklands 109, 144
on Caracciola 154
character and personality 105, 107, 128, 143,
154
death 172
describes Jack Dunfee 128
French Grand Prix (1930) 172
Le Mans (1928) 126–7, 127
Le Mans (1929) 125, 130
Le Mans (1930) 154, 156–7, 159
Le Mans (1931) 172
marriage and divorce 105, 126
and The Hon. Dorothy Paget 140, 140–41,
142–3, 144, 172
shooting prowess 105, 163
views on motor racing 143–4
Welwyn works 142, 142, 172
in World War I 105
writes autobiography (Full Throttle) 143
Blue Train run 148–51
Blume, Mary: Côte d'Azur... 148–9
B.M.W. 181
Boulogne (1923) 68
Bourne, Dale 150, 175
B.R.1 see Bentley Rotary One
B.R.2 see Bentley Rotary Two
British Automobile Racing Club (B.A.R.C.) 71
British Racing Drivers' Club 139
Brooklands 39, 40, 41, 144
Bank Holiday meeting (1928) 41
Double Twelve Hours record 54, 56
Easter Monday race (1923) 54
Essex Six Hour Race (1927) 104–5, 109
Essex Six Hour Race (1928) 125
first women's race (1927) 136
500 Miles race (1932) 176
Junior Car Club Double 12 Hour race (1930)
31
Junior Car Club 200 Mile race (1921) 41
lap record broken by Birkin 107
One Hour T.T. 18
RAC English Grand Prix (1926) 41
Spring Motor Cycle handicap (1909) 18, 18
Whitsun Meeting (1921) 42
'Brooklands Race Game' 172
'Brooklands Squad' 90, 91
Brown, Captain A.R. 22
Browning (mechanic) 49

Bruce, Hon. Victor Austin 136
Bruce, Hon. Mrs Victor (née Mary Petre) 136,
136, 138–9, 142, 178
Buchanan, Jack 98
Bugattis 49, 96, 125–6, 160

C

Callingham,
Brooklands (1927) 105
in 'Brooklands Squad' 91
Le Mans (1927) 25, 110, 116
Campbell, Malcolm 26, 89
Cannes 147, 162, 163
Carlton Hotel 148, 149, 150
Hôtel des Anglais 148
Carmichael, Sir James and Lady 148
Carraciola, Rudolf 152, 154
Belfast T.T. (1929) 156
German Grand Prix (1926) 152
Le Mans (1930) 157, 159
Casa Maury, Marquis of 49, 96
Cassel, Sir Francis 141
Chagford St, London see New Street Mews
Chanel, Coco 148–9
Chassagne, Jean 49, 125, 126–7
Clarke, 'Nobby' 22, 131, 132
Clement, Frank
on Benjafield 128
on Bentley Boys 128
on Birkin 128
Boulogne (1923) 68
Brooklands (1923) 54
Brooklands (1927) 105, 109
cartoon of 176, 177
on Duller 128
Essex Motor Club handicap race (1921) 41–2
heads Bentley's experimental department 41,
64
Isle of Man T.T. (1922) 49, 49, 51, 69
on Kidston 128
Le Mans (1923) 42, 64, 64, 65
Le Mans (1924) 54, 56
Le Mans (1927) 25, 109, 110, 119
Le Mans (1928) 127, 127
Le Mans (1929) 125
Le Mans (1930) 156, 159, 160, 162
Montlhéry record attempt (1926) 102
Coats, Jack 163
Cobb, John 89
'cocktail' racing 163
Country Life 81, 85
Couper, Mike 172
Cricklewood: Bentley factory 34, 34, 35, 36, 69

D

Daily Express 162
Daily Mail 90, 118, 173
Daimler Motor Works 26
Davis, Sidney Charles Houghton ('Sammy')
  Autocar article on Bentley road test 30–31
  and W.O. Bentley 30, 31
  Brooklands (1927) 104–5
  Brooklands (1930) *31*
  cartoon of *176*, 177
  Casque as nom de plume 24, 26
  Casques cartoons *119*
  character and personality 26, 30
  death 178, 181
  describes Barnato 101
  describes Birkin 107
  describes Brooklands committee 39
  designs team ties 156–7
  early life 26, 30
  founds Veteran Car Club of Great Britain 178
  journalistic style 143
  Le Mans (1925) 88
  Le Mans (1926) 27, 102, *104*
  Le Mans (1927) *25*, 109, 110, 112–13, 116–17, 118–19
  Le Mans (1930) 156, 159, *159*
  on methods of reviving drivers 129
  rally driving in later life 178
  in World War I 30
De Beers Consolidated Mines 82
D.F.P. (Doriet, Flandrin et Parent) sports cars *18*, *21*, *22*, *23*, 105
Don, Kaye 89, *140*
Duff, John 54
  appearance 54, *56*
  as Bentley agent 56
  Boulogne (1923) 68
  Brooklands' Double Twelve Hours' record 54, 56
  death 177
  fencing prowess 176–7
  as first Bentley Boy 26
  Indianapolis 500 Mile race (1926) *54*
  Le Mans (1923) 57, 62, 64, *64*, 65
  Le Mans (1924) 74, 75–6, *76*
  Le Mans (1925) 87, 88
  training methods 56–7
  wins Touring Grand Prix of Guipuscoa, Lasarte, Spain (1923) 67–8
  world speed record (1925) 88
  in World War I 54
du Heaume, Cyril 97, 98

Duller, George 128
  as aviator 174
  Brooklands (1927) 105
  as 'Brooklands Squad' member 90, *91*
  buys Kidston's Bugatti 126
  competes with Benjafield at Ardenrun 96
  Le Mans (1925) 88
  Le Mans (1926) 102
  Le Mans (1927) 25, 110, 116, *116*
Dunfee, Clive 98, 159, *159*. 176
Dunfee, Jack 98
  Brooklands Essex Six Hour Race (1927) 105
  cartoon of 177
  and death of brother 176
  Le Mans (1928) 127–9
  Le Mans (1929) *125*
Dunfee, Jane (née Baxter) 176
Dyhall, R. S. *91*

E

Elisabeth, Princess of Greece 148
Erlanger, Baron Gérard d' *25*, 110, *116*, *125*
Essex Motor Club 41
Essex Six Hour race *see under* Brooklands
Evening News 90
Evening Standard 163

F

Faucigny-Lucinge, Prince Jean-Louis de 148–9
Fernie, Major 21
Fiat cars 54, 56
Fletcher, Rivers 85, 97, 98
French Grand Prix
  1922 (Strasbourg) *13*
  1930 (Pau) 172

G

Gallop, Captain Clive 12, 13, *13*, 14
  at Bentley & Bentley 12, 22, 156
  and first 3-litre Bentley 12, 13, 14–15
  French Grand Prix (1922) *13*
General Strike (1926) 89, 90
Geneva Motor Salon (1982) 181
George, Prince 163
German Grand Prix (1926) 152
Gilbey, Quintin: *Queen of the Turf: The Dorothy Paget Story* 141
'Golden Miller' (horse) 177
'Grand Prix de Berkeley Square' *132*
Grand Prix de Provence (1925) 125–6
Great Depression 163, 166

Guinness, 'Bill' 49
Guipuscoa Grand Prix, Spain (1923) 67–8
Gurney Nutting 151
Gustavus V, of Sweden 148

H

Harvey, P. G. L. *91*
Hassan, Walter 56, 129, 172
Hawkes, C. 49, *49*
Hay, Michael: *Bentley Factory Cars 1919–1931* 26, 75, 163
Hélène, Grand Duchess of Russia 148
Hesse, Prince and Princess of 147
Hillstead, A.F.C.
  as Bentley Motors' salesman 34, 42, 44, 75
  Fifty Years with Motor Cars 43
  on financial situation 43–4, 75, 76
  on first Bentley customer 34, 35, 36
  at Le Mans (1923) 64
  relationship with H.M. Bentley 43
  relationship with W.O. Bentley 43, 64
  and takeover of Bentley's by Barnato 77, 85, 89, 96
  Those Bentley Days 43, 44
H.M. *see* Bentley, Horace Milner
Hogue, H.M.S. 125
Howe, Earl 138, 139, 172 cartoon of *176*, 177
Huntly, Marquess and Marchioness of 147

I

Iliffe, Sir Edward 118
Indianapolis 500 Mile race 36
  1922 47, 48, *49*
  1926 *54*
Irish T.T. races
  1922 96
  1929 129
Isaacs, Isaac 82
Isle of Man T.T. races
  1910 18
  1914 *18*, 49
  1922 42, *43*, 44, 48–9, *49*, 51

J

Joyce (driver) *54*
Juan-les-Pins 147

K

Kidston, Archie 126, 174
  affairs 175

as aviator 163, *173*, 174, *175*
Belfast T.T. (1929) 156
burnt in air crash *173*, 173–4
character and personality 126, 128, 129, 168, 178
crashes in Ulster T.T. (1928) 173
death and burial 174–6, *175*, 178
early life 125
Grand Prix de Provence (1925) 125–6
Le Mans (1929) *125*, 127, *128*
Le Mans (1930) 74, *126*, 160, 162, *162*
marriage 126
on Riviera 148, 163
Kidston, Nancy (née Soames) 126, 174, 175
King's Cup Air Race (1930) *175*
Konig, Frederick Adolphus 81
Konig, Hans Henry 81
Konig, John 78, 81

L

Lagonda 169
Lawrence, Gertrude 98
Lecoq 21
Leitzinger, Butch 182, *182*
Le Mans 24-hour races
  1923 *42*, 57, 61, 62, 64, *64*–5, 75
  1924 *56*, 64, 74, 75–6, *76*
  1925 86–8
  1926 27, 102, *102*, 104
  1927 *25*, 70, 104, *109*, 109–10, 112–13, *116*, 116–17, *117*, 118–19, *119*, 122, 125, *125*
  1928 126–7, *127*
  1929 98, *125*, 127, *128*, 130, *132*
  1930 74, 89, *154*, 156–7, *157*, 159, *159*, 160, 162, *162*
  1931 172
  2001 167–8
  2003 *181*, 182
Lillie, Beatrice 98
London to Edinburgh Trial (1906) 18

M

Mareuse, Marguerite *160*
Marina, Princess of Greece 148
Martin, Lionel 42
Mercedes 152, 154, *154*, 157, 159, 162
Mexborough, Anne, Countess of 147
Mille Miglia (1933) 172
Miniature Speedways Ltd 172
Moir, Herbert Kensington ('Bertie') and Barnato 85
  Boulogne (1923) 68

brings Benjafield into Bentley team 69–71
cartoon of 177
character and personality 49, 69
friendship with W.O. 49, 51
Isle of Man T.T. (1922) 49
at Le Mans victory dinner (1924) 76
at Le Mans (1925) 87, 88
runs Bentley service department 69, 156
Montlhéry racetrack, France 88, 102, 136, *136*, 138–9
Motor, The 42, 88, 117
Mountbatten, Lord Louis 125
Mussolini, Benito 172

N

Nash, Frazer 90
New Street Mews, London (*later* Chagford Street) 10, 12–13, *14*, 21
Newton, Ernest: Ardenrun 82
Nicholas, Princess of Greece 148
Nürburgring circuit, Germany (1928) 154

O

Orloff, Madame 141

P

Paget, The Hon. Dorothy Paget appearance 141
  aversion to men 141
  and Birkin *140*, 140–41, 142–3, 144, 156, 172
  death 178
  as gambler 141
  and motor-racing 141, 142, 144, 178
  nocturnal existence in later years 177–8
  obituary 144
  as successful racehorse owner 141, 177
Paris Motor Salon (1930) 151
Pennal, Leslie *44*, 49
Phoenix Park, Dublin 144
Poele, Eric van de 182, *182*
Porter, George 49
Puss Moth aircraft 163, 174, *175*

Q

Quadrant motorcycles 18
Queenborough, Almeric Paget, Lord 141

R

R.A.C. 150
Ramponi, Giulio *159*
Rex motorcycles 18, *18*
Rhodes, Cecil 82–3
Richmond and Gordon, Charles Gordon-Lennox (Lord Settrington), Duke of 30, 128
  cartoon 177
Richthofen, Manfred von 22
Rizzo, M. 90
Rolls-Royce(s) 36, 44, 141, 144, 167, 169, 172, 181
  Silver Ghost 75
Rossmere, Lord *91*
Royal Flying Corps 12, 13
Rubin, Bernard
  as aviator 174
  and Barnato 125, 148
  Belfast T.T. (1929) 156
  and Birkin 156, 172
  death 176
  drinking habit 129
  Essex Six Hour race (1928) 125
  Le Mans (1928) 127
  marriage 176
  Mille Miglia (1933) 172
  wounded in war 125
Rubinstein, Mark 125

S

Sallon, Ralph: Bentley Boys cartoons *176*, 177
Saunders 49, 130
Scarsdale, Viscount and Viscountess 148
Segrave, Henry 49, 88, 90, *91*
  Brooklands (1927) 105
Selby-Lowness, Colonel 90
Settrington, Lord *see* Richmond and Gordon, Duke of
Shadwell Court, Norfolk 142, 163
Shaw, Norman 82
Sheffield, Edmund 175
Siko, Odette *160*
Simmons, Sir Percy 148
Six Days Trial (Wales, 1909) 18
Sketch 163
Sopwith Camels *20*, 22
Sphere magazine 98
Sporting Life 89, 144
Straker-Squire 49
Sunbeams 49, 88, 102, 105
Sunday Times 49

INDEX AND ACKNOWLEDGEMENTS

T

Tacolneston Hall, Norfolk 105, 142
Tatler magazine 98
Temperley, Commander 91
Thrupp and Maberly: Standard Six 98
Tomlinson, Lawrence 182
Tourist Trophy (T.T.) races 1909 18
   Belfast (1929) 156
   Brooklands One Hour 18
   Ulster (1928) 173
   see also Irish T.T.; Isle of Man T.T.
Tripoli Grand Prix (1933) 172

U

Ulster T.T. (1928) 173

V

Van Raalte, Noel 34, 35–6, 37
Veteran Car Club of Great Britain 178
Volkswagen Group 181, 182

W

Walker, Diana Barnato 151, 182
Wall Street Crash (1929) 132
Wallace, Andy *182*
Watney, Richard *159*, *160*
Westminster, Hugh Grosvenor, 2nd Duke of 148
White, Captain 'Babe' 163
Whitney, Pauline (Lady Queenborough) 141
Windsor, Duke of 107
W.O. *see* Bentley, Walter Owen
Wood, Beris Harcourt 156
World War I 13, 14, 21–2, 30, 54, 125
   women in 136

Z

Zborowski, Count 41

Acknowledgements

We are grateful to the following for permission to reproduce photographs:

AKG page 155a; Alamy106; Robert Benjafield pages 67, 68, 71; Bentley Media pages 33, 57, 64, 89, 157, 183; British Pathe pages 87, 130a,b,c, 131; Brooklands Motoring Museum pages 55, 56, 155b; Daily Mirror page 91b; Nicholas Foulkes Archive pages 118, 177; Getty pages 135, 137, 154, 168; Mark Goodman Archive page 100; Hertfordshire County Council pages 141, 142; © Hulton-Deutsch Collection/CORBIS pages 2, 22, 52–53, 169; Illustrated London News pages 140, 146, 163b; Hugo Kidston Archive pages 73, 124, 126, 129, 133, 162, 163a, 166–167, 170–171, 175; Simon Kidston Archive pages 173, 179; John Konig Archive pages 80, 81, 83; LAT Photographic pages 12, 13, 27, 28–29, 38, 40–41, 61, 76, 94–95, 158, 159, 160, 161; Simon Lewis page 145; National Motor Museum, Beaulieu pages 17b, 43a, 84, 99, 123, 130d; Michael Russell Archive page 37.

We would like to thank the W.O. Bentley Memorial Foundation for granting permission to reproduce photographs from the archive of the Bentley Drivers' Club.

Every effort has been made to trace the copyright holders of material used in this publication. However, we have been unable to trace some copyright holders and would be grateful for any information that will enable us to do so.

Clement and Chassagne make a quick change over (overleaf) during the 1929 Le Mans.